Making and Unmaking Refugees

This book examines the politics of making and unmaking refugees at various scales by probing the contradictions between the principles of international statecraft, which focus on the national/state level approach in regulating global forced displacement, and the forces that defy this state-based approach. It explores the ways by which the current global refugee categorizes and excludes millions of people who need protection. The investigations in this book move beyond the state scale to draw attention to the finer scales of displacement and forced mobility in the various, complex spaces of migration and asylum. By bringing refugees stories to the forefront, the chapters in this volume highlight diasporic activism and applaud the corresponding ingenuity and tenacity. This book also builds upon debates on the critical geopolitical understandings of states, displacement and bordering to advance theoretical understandings of refugee regimes as a critical geopolitical issue. With this collection, the contributors invite a more sustained conversation that draws attention to and focusses on the current global refugee crisis and the violence of exclusion of that same regime.

This highly engaging and informative volume will be of interest to policymakers, academics and students concerned with global migration, refugee governance and crises. The chapters in this book were originally published as a special issue of *Geopolitics*.

Kara E. Dempsey is Associate Professor at Appalachian State University. She is a political geographer that studies ethnonational conflicts, consolidation of state and regional power, international forced migration, and peace-building processes. She is the author of *The Geopolitics of Conflict, Nationalism, and Reconciliation in Ireland* (Routledge, 2022). She currently is serving as the president of the Political Geography Specialty Group, American Association of Geographers.

Orhon Myadar is Associate Professor at University of Arizona. She is a political geographer interested in questions of power, ideology, mobility and identity within the context of shifting political landscapes. She is the author of *Mobility and Displacement: Nomadism, Identity and Post-Colonial Narratives in Mongolia* (Routledge, 2021).

Making and Unmaking Refugees
Geopolitics of Social Ordering and Struggle within the Global Refugee Regime

Edited by
Kara E. Dempsey and Orhon Myadar

LONDON AND NEW YORK

First published 2023
by Routledge
4 Park Square, Milton Park, Abingdon, Oxon OX14 4RN

and by Routledge
605 Third Avenue, New York, NY 10158

Routledge is an imprint of the Taylor & Francis Group, an informa business

Introduction, Chapters 1–5 © 2023 Taylor & Francis

All rights reserved. No part of this book may be reprinted or reproduced or utilised in any form or by any electronic, mechanical, or other means, now known or hereafter invented, including photocopying and recording, or in any information storage or retrieval system, without permission in writing from the publishers.

Trademark notice: Product or corporate names may be trademarks or registered trademarks, and are used only for identification and explanation without intent to infringe.

British Library Cataloguing in Publication Data
A catalogue record for this book is available from the British Library

ISBN13: 978-1-032-45270-8 (hbk)
ISBN13: 978-1-032-45271-5 (pbk)
ISBN13: 978-1-003-37621-7 (ebk)

DOI: 10.4324/9781003376217

Typeset in Garamond
by Newgen Publishing UK

Publisher's Note
The publisher accepts responsibility for any inconsistencies that may have arisen during the conversion of this book from journal articles to book chapters, namely the inclusion of journal terminology.

Disclaimer
Every effort has been made to contact copyright holders for their permission to reprint material in this book. The publishers would be grateful to hear from any copyright holder who is not here acknowledged and will undertake to rectify any errors or omissions in future editions of this book.

Contents

Citation Information vi
Notes on Contributors viii

Introduction—Making and Unmaking Refugees: Geopolitics of
Social Ordering and Struggle within the Global Refugee Regime 1
Orhon Myadar and Kara E. Dempsey

1 The Shifting Landscape of International Resettlement: Canada,
the US and Syrian Refugees 9
Pablo S. Bose

2 Migrant Agency and Counter-Hegemonic Efforts Among Asylum
Seekers in the Netherlands in Response to Geopolitical Control and
Exclusion 36
Kara E. Dempsey

3 Diaspora Geopolitics in Toronto: Tamil Nationalism and the
Aftermath of War in Sri Lanka 58
*Jennifer Hyndman, Amarnath Amarasingam and
Gayathri Naganathan*

4 Geopoliticizing Geographies of Care: Scales of Responsibility
Towards Sea-borne Migrants and Refugees in the Mediterranean 78
Sara McDowell

5 Place, Displacement and Belonging: The Story of Abdi 96
Orhon Myadar

Index 112

Citation Information

The chapters in this book were originally published in the journal *Geopolitics*, volume 27, issue 2 (2022). When citing this material, please use the original page numbering for each article, as follows:

Introduction
Making and Unmaking Refugees: Geopolitics of Social Ordering and Struggle within the Global Refugee Regime
Orhon Myadar and Kara E. Dempsey
Geopolitics, volume 27, issue 2 (2022), pp. 367–374

Chapter 1
The Shifting Landscape of International Resettlement: Canada, the US and Syrian Refugees
Pablo S. Bose
Geopolitics, volume 27, issue 2 (2022), pp. 375–401

Chapter 2
Migrant Agency and Counter-Hegemonic Efforts Among Asylum Seekers in the Netherlands in Response to Geopolitical Control and Exclusion
Kara E. Dempsey
Geopolitics, volume 27, issue 2 (2022), pp. 402–423

Chapter 3
Diaspora Geopolitics in Toronto: Tamil Nationalism and the Aftermath of War in Sri Lanka
Jennifer Hyndman, Amarnath Amarasingam and Gayathri Naganathan
Geopolitics, volume 27, issue 2 (2022), pp. 424–443

Chapter 4
Geopoliticizing Geographies of Care: Scales of Responsibility Towards Sea-borne Migrants and Refugees in the Mediterranean
Sara McDowell
Geopolitics, volume 27, issue 2 (2022), pp. 444–461

Chapter 5
Place, Displacement and Belonging: The Story of Abdi
Orhon Myadar
Geopolitics, volume 27, issue 2 (2022), pp. 462–477

For any permission-related enquiries please visit:
www.tandfonline.com/page/help/permissions

Notes on Contributors

Amarnath Amarasingam, School of Religion, Queens University, Kingston, Ontario, Canada.

Pablo S. Bose, Department of Geography, University of Vermont, Burlington, USA.

Kara E. Dempsey, Department of Geography and Planning, Appalachian State University, Boone, North Carolina, USA.

Jennifer Hyndman, Centre for Refugee Studies, York University, Toronto, Canada.

Sara McDowell, School of Geography and Environmental Sciences, Ulster University, Coleraine, Northern Ireland.

Orhon Myadar, School of Geography, Development and Environment, University of Arizona, Tucson, AZ, USA.

Gayathri Naganathan, Department of Surgery, University of Toronto, Ontario, Canada.

Introduction—Making and Unmaking Refugees: Geopolitics of Social Ordering and Struggle within the Global Refugee Regime

Orhon Myadar and Kara E. Dempsey

Wars and conflicts around the world take the lives of millions and leave millions more displaced both physically and emotionally. With an unprecedented number of displaced peoples worldwide, the plight of refugees, stateless, and internally-displaced people remains a crucial global issue. The current COVID-19 pandemic and subsequent growth of restrictions and barriers to mobility and resettlement have further exacerbated the challenges faced by displaced persons.

Recent and emerging geographic scholarship has paid considerable attention to the interlocking themes of mobility, borders, immigration and displacement as critical to understanding the current global refugee crisis. *Geopolitics*, in particular, has featured several themed issues and sections that attend to the various ways borders and bordering practices shape and inform migration, mobility and displacement. In 1998, then-editor David Newman organised a special issue on *Boundaries and Territories and Postmodernity*. This plenary special issue focused on the 'new world order' and the extent to which borders have become increasingly permeable in the post-Westphalian geopolitical context. The special issue also called for continued engagement with the subject of changing territorial orderings (Newman 1998).

Over the last two decades, *Geopolitics* has sustained the conversation through special issues and sections on themes related to borders, mobility and migration (Varsanyi and Nevins 2007; Hyndman 2012; Dell'Agnese and Szary 2015; Mainwaring and Brigden 2016; Beurskens and Miggelbrink 2017; Makarychev 2018; Meier 2018). However, while some special issues/sections have examined refugees within the context of broader discussions of migration and mobility, there have been no themed issues solely devoted to the geopolitics of refugee categorisations and various forms of violence experienced by globally-displaced persons within the global refugee regime.

This themed special section brings the intersection of embodied experiences and social ordering produced by the global refugee regime to the forefront through a collection of original articles that engage both theoretical and empirical examinations of the global crisis. Examining the geopolitics of *"making and unmaking refugees"* provides us with an analytical lens to better problematise the ambiguous, bureaucratically-ominous, and often politically-charged categorisation of persons who are displaced (see for instance Jones 2016) as 'refugees.' As such, this collection endeavours to draw attention to the slipperiness of such categorisation and how it haphazardly designates, hierarchises, legitimatises and delegitimizes those who are displaced because of forces beyond their control. We recognise that while the refugee classification affords safety and security to some, the same classification leads to the exclusion and deprivation of basic rights to millions of others.

Who is a refugee? And who decides whether one is a refugee or not? What is behind the label, and what implications does the label carry for those it designates and those it does not?

Etymologically, the term 'refugee' comes from the French word *réfugié*, meaning 'to seek refuge.' It was first used to describe French Huguenots who fled France to escape religious persecution following the revocation of the Edict of Nantes in 1685.[1] The internationally-accepted legal definition of 'refugee' was adopted by the 1951 Refugee Convention to provide protections to those fleeing persecution. But the scope of the original Convention was limited geographically to Europe, a region that was still reeling from the violence of World War II. Temporally, it was also limited to those events occurring before January 1, 1951 (UN General Assembly 1967). These restrictions were later removed by the 1967 Protocol to cover refugees universally in a period in which decolonisation efforts and Cold-War conflicts uprooted people from their homelands across the world.

A refugee is legally defined today as someone who is 'unable or unwilling to return to their country of origin owing to a well-founded fear of being persecuted for reasons of race, religion, nationality, membership of a particular social group, or political opinion' (Ibid). As this definition emphasises political and other forms of persecution as the conditions that compel individuals to flee their home countries, it excludes millions of individuals who are displaced because of other life-threatening conditions, such as natural calamities, from refugee designation. This rigid categorisation of displaced persons continues to produce social bodies whose fates are routinely determined by the assumption of sovereign borders and the exclusionary ontology upon which borders are predicated (e.g., Dempsey 2020; Hiemstra 2019; Myadar 2020). As such, the current global refugee regime has excluded more uprooted individuals from its mandated protection than it has included.

At the heart of the process of making and unmaking refugees is therefore the politics of labelling and categorisation that institutionalise the global refugee regime and social capacities the labelling dictates in return. As Gupte and Mehta (2007, 22) suggest, labels are assumed as 'objective, efficient, routine, and indispensable ... and [are therefore] consequential when enforced by authoritative state agents.' Labels sustain 'a recursive relationship with policy-making processes in that they are tools to aid such processes which themselves have bearing on how labels are formed, and what meaning they hold' (Ibid). But beyond the veneer of administrative objectivity, the categorisation of people through labels allows radically different outcomes for those differently labelled by given bureaucratic formulae.

In understanding the social ordering created by the global refugee regime, Tazreena Sajjad (2018) provides a useful insight. According to Sajjad (2018), the consequence of labelling who is a refugee and who is not ultimately defines "the experience of forcible displacement into a one-dimensional status that both captures a specific moment in time, and crafts the individual as being ahistorical and neutral in relationship to a (benevolent) state." Yet, labels have "immense personal, political and practical significance associated with productive and prescriptive capacities" (Sajjad 2018, 46). Labels such as 'refugee,' 'economic migrant' and 'illegal migrant,' for example, carry particular sets of assumptions that narrow the political and social capacities of those so labelled (Ibid). One who is categorised as a refugee is seen as deserving of protection, while one who is excluded from the category is often commodified as an economic migrant or not deserving of the protection of basic human rights (Sajjad 2018).

The categorisation of displaced persons as refugees or not refugees is ultimately rooted in and governed by the state-based system of global governance. Globally-displaced populations have been forced to negotiate their fates within and across the system that is predicated upon what Hannah Arendt (1951, 282) refers to as 'the old trinity of state-people-territory.' The hegemonic structure and power relations produced by the global order of the nation-state determine the hierarchy of protection of globally-displaced persons.

In exploring the politics of making and unmaking refugees, the collection of papers in this issue thus probes the contradictions between the principles of international statecraft that are predicated upon the based on the sanctity of states, and the forces that defy the assumption. The state-centred approach fails to attend to intimate, embodied, affective and emotional landscapes in understanding and problematising the effects of the regulation of forcibly displaced peoples (e.g., Hakli and Kallio 2014; Hiemstra 2019; Hyndman 2019; Koopman 2011; Mountz and Hyndman 2006). By de-centring the state and challenging the traditional production of geopolitical knowledge, this section draws attention to the intimate and finer scales of displacement and forced mobility (e.g., Dempsey 2020; McNevin 2019; Shindo 2019; Vayrynen et al. 2017)

The special section both engages and challenges the asymmetry of power embedded in the state-centred world order in an effort to situate the ongoing, slow and visceral violence experienced by globally-displaced persons and to elucidate the intimate and embodied geographies such violence produces. By doing so, we also highlight the power of human agency and collective activism to challenge, subvert or otherwise negotiate the symbolic and physical grids of borders, surveillance and control within the global world order.

Building upon and contributing to the debates on the critical geopolitical understandings of states, displacement and bordering, this special section aims to advance our theoretical understandings of refugee regimes as a critical geopolitical issue by addressing the following questions:

- How does the current global refugee regime contribute to the process of making and unmaking refugees? How can scholarly attention to the processes of making and unmaking refugees help elucidate the violence and power of the state-centred global order regulating migrant bodies? How are these individuals shaped by the geopolitical framings of migrants and refugees?
- How do migrants counter, challenge, and resist sovereign hegemony that excludes, regulates and surveils them within this process that designates them as (un)worthy?
- How does sovereign hegemony shape the geographies of care and responsibility? In designating who is a refugee or who is not, how do states allocate 'humanitarian' efforts to those who are in need?
- In understanding the process of (un)making refugees, how do we understand the interim zones such as asylum camps as well as diaspora politics?
- How do we situate the "self" within the processes of the broader global refugee regime? How do we unpack the relationships among place, belonging, and self when one is violently displaced?

These questions collectively probe the process of making and unmaking refugees and how this process manifests at various scales, from the international refugee regime to rescue boats to asylum camps to the intimate scale of the self. Each scale offers a particular window into the ways the current global refugee regime legitimatises and delegitimizes those who are displaced because of forces beyond their control, hierarchising human lives according to superficial rules that are predicated upon the sanctity of states.

The section begins with Bose's paper that investigates the hegemonic structure and power relations produced by the state-centred global order and its implications for the making and unmaking of refugees. Through his analysis of the responses by the Canadian and US federal governments to the Syrian refugee crisis in 2015, Bose demonstrates how a complex grid of domestic and international policies continue to define social bodies to be included or excluded within national sovereign borders and how by doing so these policies routinely define who is a refugee and who is not. Canada resettled nearly 55,000 individuals through its refugee programme in the two years since the Syrian war started, while the US progressively cut its acceptance of Syrian refugees to nearly zero during the same period.[2] Yet, despite the disparity between the US and Canadian responses to the current refugee crisis, the primacy of national interests continues to outweigh each state's international and humanitarian commitment to assist refugees. As Bose demonstrates, while the need for sanctuary and protection is as great (or greater) than ever, the Covid-19 pandemic has allowed a number of states to achieve what would have otherwise been unthinkable – shutting the door on refugee resettlement as a key pillar of international law and protection.

Dempsey's paper provides geographies of forced migration within the EU as a lens through which we can understand the complex process of making and unmaking refugees. It explores intersections between politics and political subjectivities enacted by forced migrants within the Dutch asylum system. Within this murky process of un(making) refugees, these migrants experience processes of displacement, state-surveillance, alienation and vulnerability as their legal status restricts their mobility and postpones employment. However, her research illuminates, in spite of this regime of state control and surveillance, migrants challenge and subvert the hierarchical control of everyday spaces and the embodied geopolitical violence in asylum camps. Drawing from original fieldwork, Dempsey examines various Dutch asylum camps as a site of generative struggle, the intersection of key forms of geopolitical control of asylum seekers (e.g., surveillance, categorisation, segregation, and exclusion), with that of migrant agency, counter-hegemonic efforts, and networks that are forged, grounded in and stretched beyond asylum camp borders.

Hyndman, Amarasingam, and Naganathan's paper further illustrates migrant agency and collective activism. The authors' examination of the Sri Lankan Tamil diaspora in Canada offers a unique vantage point to understand the complex process of making and unmaking refugees. The authors examine the tale of migrants on a broader arc of time and space beyond the border regime that allows or denies migrants' entrance into a particular sovereign space. Drawing on interviews and focus groups with members of the Sri Lankan Tamil diaspora in Canada, the authors argue that examining diaspora activism primarily through the prism of securitisation and extremism flattens understanding of diaspora activism and how it evolves over time. Understanding the diverse relations that members of this community have with the militarised violence in Sri Lanka requires that scholars and policymakers move beyond the securitisation discourse and look more closely at the ways in which transnational activism is increasingly rooted in frameworks of international law, human rights, and social justice.

In her paper, McDowell demonstrates how different meanings are provided for those who are included or excluded within the sovereign-based framings of the world order. She does so by specifically focusing within a frame of duty and care afforded to those who are considered deserving of a state's duty and care and denied from those who are excluded from such basic human rights. As

McDowell demonstrates, geographies of care and responsibility are becoming more limited, focusing on the immediate needs of those on the 'inside' or who are perceived to belong. She allows readers to zoom into the operation of the humanitarian vessel Aquarius, a ship that intercepts sea-borne migrants in distress in the Mediterranean. McDowell's analysis of search and rescue activities (SAR) in the Mediterranean urges us to think about the ways in which geographies of care and responsibility intersect and collide with the geopolitical framing of how people are categorised as refugees, migrants or illegals. She suggests that through unpacking the legislative and ethical frameworks shaping SAR activities in the Mediterranean, we can observe a distinct 'geopoliticizing of care and responsibility' whereby these individuals become pawns in wider power dynamics within the European Union.

To bring our affective and intimate understanding of globally-displaced persons to the forefront, Myadar's paper focuses on a story of single person, Abdi, who trekked his way from Migwa, Somalia to Tucson, Arizona. Inspired by Chimamanda Ngozi Adichie's concept of the power of a single story, the article zooms into the lived story of one person's journey as he navigated the processes of making and unmaking him a refugee within a broader international refugee regime. In some ways, Abdi's journey illustrates the uncanny ways the global order operates, how this order makes and unmakes refugees, and how this process is as unpredictable and treacherous as the road Abdi took to flee from violence in his village. Abdi's story also symbolises human agency and the individual's power to negotiate, counter, subvert or otherwise reorient geopolitical orderings to the most intimate scale of geography: the self.

Indeed, this collection contributes to investigations of refugees and forced mobility by shifting the focus away from a solely governance perspective in order to draw attention to intimate and finer scales – including the scale of the self. We highlight diasporic activism and applaud the ingenuity and tenacity of refugees by bringing their stories to the forefront. Our scholarly accounts examine the processes of (un)making of refugees via the exclusionary hierarchies of bureaucratic administration and the biased, often politically-charged categorisations that exist in the various, complex spaces of migration and asylum.

With this collection, we invite more sustained conversations that draw attention to and focus on the current global refugee crisis. We hope these conversations will continue to draw attention not only to the violence that drives people away from their homelands but also the violence of exclusion of the current global refugee regime.

Notes

1. For more on the exodus of refugee Huguenots see, Golden (1988).
2. This trend is expected to reverse with Biden administration pledging to increase the annual cap of refugee admissions to 125,000 (The White House 2021).

ORCID

Orhon Myadar http://orcid.org/0000-0002-0372-2960

References

Arendt, H. 1951. *The origins of totalitarianism*. New York: Schocken Books.
Beurskens, K., and J. Miggelbrink. 2017. Special section introduction–Sovereignty contested: Theory and practice in borderlands. *Geopolitics* 22 (4):749–56. doi:10.1080/14650045.2017.1373582.
Dell'Agnese, E., and A. A. Szary. 2015. Borderscapes: From border landscapes to border aesthetics. *Geopolitics* 20 (1):4–13. doi:10.1080/14650045.2015.1014284.
Dempsey, K. E. 2020. Spaces of violence: A typology of the political geography of violence against migrants seeking asylum in the EU. *Political Geography* 79:102157. doi:10.1016/j.polgeo.2020.102157.
Golden, R. M., ed. 1988. *The huguenot connection: The edict of Nantes, its revocation, and early French migration to South Carolina*. Vol. 125. Dordrecht: Kluwer Academic Publishers.
Gupte, J., and L. Mehta. 2007. Disjunctures in labelling refugees and oustees. In *The power of labelling: How people are categorized and why it matters*, ed. J. Moncrieffe and R. Eyben, 64–79. London: Earthscan.
Hakli, J., and K. Kallio. 2014. Subject, action and polis: Theorizing political agency. *Progress in Human Geography* 38 (2):181–200. doi:10.1177/0309132512473869.
Hiemstra, N. 2019. *Detain and deport: The chaotic US immigration enforcement regime*. Athens: University of Georgia.
Hyndman, J. 2012. The geopolitics of migration and mobility. *Geopolitics* 17 (2):243–55. doi:10.1080/14650045.2011.569321.
Hyndman, J. 2019. Unsettling feminist geopolitics: Forging feminist political geographies of violence. *Gender, Place and Culture* 26:3–29. doi:10.1080/0966369X.2018.1561427.
Jones, R. 2016. *Violent borders: Refugees and the right to move*. Brooklyn: Verso Books.
Koopman, S. 2011. Alter-geopolitics: Other securities are happening. *Geoforum* 42:274–84. doi:10.1016/j.geoforum.2011.01.007.
Makarychev, A. 2018. Bordering and identity-making in Europe after the 2015 refugee crisis. *Geopolitics* 23 (4):747–53. doi:10.1080/14650045.2018.1499380.
McNevin, A. 2019. Mobility and its discontents: Seeing beyond international space and progressive time. *Environment and Planning C: Politics and Space* (August):2019. doi:10.1177/2399654419871966.
Meier, D. 2018. Introduction to the special issue: Bordering the Middle East. *Geopolitics* 23 (3):495–504. doi:10.1080/14650045.2018.1497375.
Mountz, A., and J. Hyndman. 2006. Feminist approaches to the global intimate. *Women's Studies Quarterly* 34 (1–2):446–63.
Myadar, O. 2020. *Mobility and displacement: Nomadism, identity and postcolonial narratives in Mongolia*. London and New York: Routledge.
Mainwaring, Ċ. and Brigden, N., 2016. Beyond the border: Clandestine migration journeys. Geopolitics. 243–262.
Newman, D. 1998. Geopolitics renaissant: Territory, sovereignty and the world political map. *Geopolitics* 3 (1):1–16. doi:10.1080/14650049808407604.
Sajjad, T. 2018. What's in a name? 'Refugees', 'migrants' and the politics of labelling. *Race & Class* 60 (2):40–62. doi:10.1177/0306396818793582.

Shindo, R. 2019. *Belonging in translation: Solidarity and migrant activism in Japan*. Bristol: Bristol University Press.
UN General Assembly. 1967. Protocol relating to the status of refugees. *Treaty Series* 606. Accessed August 8, 2020. https://www.unhcr.org/3b66c2aa10.html
Varsanyi, M. W., and J. Nevins. 2007. Introduction: Borderline contradictions: Neoliberalism, unauthorised migration, and intensifying immigration policing. *Geopolitics* 12 (2):223–27. doi:10.1080/14650040601168800.
Vayrynen, T., E. Puumala, S. Pehkonen, A. Kynsilehto, and T. Vaittinen. 2017. *Choreographies or resistance: Mobile bodies and relational politics*. London: Rowman & Littlefield.
The White House. 2021. Executive order on rebuilding and enhancing programs to resettle refugees and planning for the impact of climate change on migration. Accessed February 12, 2021. https://www.whitehouse.gov/briefing-room/presidential-actions/2021/02/04/executive-order-on-rebuilding-and-enhancing-programs-to-resettle-refugees-and-planning-for-the-impact-of-climate-change-on-migration/.

The Shifting Landscape of International Resettlement: Canada, the US and Syrian Refugees

Pablo S. Bose

ABSTRACT
The world is today in the grip of the worst forced migration crisis since the end of the Second World War, with tens of millions driven from their homes by conflict. Yet the global system meant to provide protection to the displaced continues to privilege the interests of nation-states rather than those of refugees and has resulted in less willingness by many countries to accept refugees for resettlement. The arrival – actual or potential – of large numbers of refugees and asylum seekers continues to spur a backlash against them, fuelled by fears of security threats, economic costs, and a lack of integration of newcomers. This situation has combined with xenophobia, racism, and broader cultural anxieties and led to a rising tide of nativist populism and even less welcome for those seeking sanctuary. Whereas by the late 1990 s the dominant logic governing refugee protections – at least in name if not in practice – was centred on multilateralism and humanitarian obligations, today there is a more explicit prominence of national interests in refugee policies. In this paper I argue that the continued dominance of nation-state centric priorities is indicative of the fragility of the global refugee regime. I use the example of Canadian and US responses to the Syrian refugee crisis and interviews with officials in each country to illustrate the primacy of national interests rather than international agreements and norms. The US chose to limit and eventually bar most Syrians from resettlement whereas Canada chose to accept a large number over a short period of time. I argue that both cases reveal similar patterns and logics, if not outcomes and an increasing alignment between border controls and immigration policy. I consider what this means for the future of refugee resettlement in North America and for the global refugee regime more broadly.

Introduction

The global community is today confronted by one of the worst refugee crises since the end of the Second World War, with millions of people displaced from homes and livelihoods. The numbers have swelled dramatically in the past decade – in 2010 there were approximately 34 million people who were counted as forcibly displaced; today over 70 million people fill those categories (UNHCR, 2020). While the need for protection may have increased, the capacity and willingness of many state actors to provide sanctuary has moved in the opposite direction. This is especially true for wealthier countries in the Global North, many of which have progressively reduced the numbers of refugees they have been willing to resettle in recent years. Security concerns, rising xenophobia and nativism, demographic change, political radicalization and polarization are just some of the factors that have exacerbated these trends.

Yet the shift towards greater securitization of migration is not simply a product of the current environment; it points instead to deeper and more long-term fragilities in and evolutions of the global refugee and resettlement systems that have been occurring for at least several decades. While refugee protection is often framed by advocates and multilateral organizations as a commitment to international humanitarian obligations, historically it has more often been shaped by the interests of particular nation-states – especially foreign policy goals and domestic immigration debates. Such a dynamic is especially true today as national refugee policies increasingly – or at least more explicitly – become part of a broader set of conversations regarding borders, citizenship, immigration, integration and cultural change the world over. I argue in this paper that what we see on display in today's acceptance and/or rejection of refugees by individual nation states is a more explicit acknowledgement in the global refugee regime of something that has long been true: the primacy of *national immigration interests* over *international migration policy*.

I examine this dynamic through a comparison of US and Canadian government responses to the exodus of Syrian refugees due to civil war and ongoing instability. In particular, I look at the ways in which some of those most involved with refugee resettlement in Canada and the US – government officials, social service providers and community members among them – understand the objectives, politics and outcomes of the approach to Syrian refugees taken in each country. On the surface the two sets of responses seem polar opposites. In 2015, the Canadian government committed to accepting 25,000 refugees (Government of Canada 2017) and having quickly reached that goal has gone on to accept a total of 54,560 Syrian refugees (IRCC, 2019). In the US, on the other hand, after the Obama administration initially committed to accepting 10,000 Syrian refugees in 2016 and a further 30,000 in 2017, the Trump administration reversed this course in 2017 and through a series of travel bans and restrictions on security clearance and admissions ended up effectively barring most Syrian refugees from coming to the US.

I draw on interviews with key informants involved with resettlement in each country to explore the reasons behind these two differing outcomes. In both cases, my respondents suggest that domestic politics regarding immigration and struggles over national identity continue to play an outsize role in shaping refugee policies in each country. For scholars of international relations and especially global refugee policies, such a realization may not come as a surprise. But my interviews revealed that for longtime civil servants engaged in refugee work in these two countries, the idea that humanitarian ideals might be supplanted by national self-interest did in fact appear to come as a shock, highlighting the fact that for large parts of the global refugee regime a belief in multilateralism in migration policy might indeed be deeply embedded.

My interviews focus in particular on ones conducted between 2013 and 2018 and highlight the significance of two particular national election cycles in each country. In Canada, the momentum to resettle a large number of Syrian refugees became enmeshed in the 2015 Canadian general election, with the victorious Liberal Party headed by Justin Trudeau making the acceptance of Syrians a central part of its election platform. In the US, the opposite was true, with Donald Trump making the rejection of Syrians an important part of *his* winning presidential campaign in 2016.

The outcomes of these national elections and the centrality of a particular refugee crisis to each is not simply about the significance of domestic interests vis-à-vis refugee policies. Rather, they illuminate the fragility of the international system of refugee protections and how reactive it is to local and domestic politics and to national self-interest. This is not a new trend; anxieties regarding immigration, demographics, and cultural change have long underscored refugee policies not only in the US and Canada, but in many other countries around the world. In the current moment, however, such anxieties – if not outright xenophobia and anti-immigrant sentiment – have been made explicit in refugee policies and the treatment of those seeking sanctuary. This has resulted in a movement away from the discourses of protection, international obligations and human rights that had become dominant by the late 1990 s – at least amongst many of those most intimately involved with resettlement – to ones that today increasingly privilege national security, economic costs and benefits, and cultural homogeneity.

I examine this dynamic by beginning with a brief overview of the contemporary moment in refugee flows and resettlement patterns. I then turn to the specific context of forced migration from Syria and the US and Canadian responses to this situation. The rest of the paper focuses on how these responses have been structured by domestic political situations and interests, especially as articulated by key actors within each country's respective refugee resettlement apparatus. Taken together, these two cases suggest that despite differing outcomes, there is a continued and growing dependency of the global refugee system on national interests and domestic priorities regarding immigration rather than international obligations and multilateral commitments.

The Global Forced Migration Crisis and the Politics of Refugee Resettlement

Between 2015 and 2019, the number of refugees worldwide spiked to levels not seen in decades (UNHCR, 2020). Civil wars, ethnic conflicts, oppression of groups based on religion, ethnicity, gender, sexuality or other forms of identity and natural disasters are among the reasons that so many people are currently on the move, whether within their own countries or across a border. Not all of those who are displaced are recognized or afforded protections by the international community – those affected by the building of a dam or by rising sea levels, for example, are not recognized as official refugees (Penz, Drydyk, and Bose 2011). If we counted these other groups of forced migrants, potentially tens of millions more would be added to the lists of those in need. Yet even if we continue to limit our view of refugees only to those who have been affected by conflict and persecution, the trend towards a growing number of displaced is unlikely to abate any time soon. Ongoing wars in Syria and Yemen and conflicts in the Ukraine, South Sudan, the Democratic Republic of Congo and Myanmar to name but a few examples, continue to produce refugees at an alarming rate (OCHA 2019; Ullah and Roy Choudhury 2018).

The global refugee regime that has developed to address such situations has its roots in the post-WWII period and in accords such as the 1948 UN Human Rights Agreement and the 1951 UN Refugee Convention, designed initially and primarily to address masses of displaced persons in Europe (Betts and Loescher, 2011). Such agreements have at their core several central beliefs: that all people are deserving of protection under international law from harm, that they have the right to return to their homes once the conflict ends and that they should not be forced to return if the conditions that displaced them in the first place have not improved. There are different ways to enter the global refugee protection system – those who are able to can hopefully find shelter in a refugee camp and be granted official recognition and status. If conditions in their home countries improve, the hope is that they will be able to return and rebuild their lives. But for many such an outcome is unlikely. For some a protracted stay in the camp occurs – for many Bhutanese and Somali refugees, for example, entire generations have lived, died and been born in foreign camps (Devictor and Do, 2017).

A miniscule proportion of those seeking protection end up becoming permanently resettled in wealthier countries of the Global North – of the over 70 million 'persons of concern' to the UNHCR in 2018, just over 92,000 were actually resettled as refugees (UNHCR, 2019). As Bradley points out, "only a tiny minority of refugees (typically the most well-educated and the wealthiest, relatively speaking) have the opportunity to seek asylum or acquire citizenship in the affluent, multicultural democracies (Bradley 2014, 104). Such resettlement means travel to an often-distant country with integration, permanent residence and perhaps citizenship as hoped-for outcomes. I focus in this paper on this small but significant part of the global refugee regime. I do so because refugees (or the possibility of refugees) have in recent years had a disproportionate influence on the forced migration policies of so-called third countries in the Global North. While it is in countries of the Global South that the vast majority of forced migrants actually reside in camps or other forms of shelter, much of the world's focus has been on refugees and their reception in countries in North America and Europe.

This is perhaps not surprising, not only due to the relative power of the Global North vis-à-vis the rest of the world, but because the global refugee regime has from its outset been focused on this region. Yet the limitations of WWII-era refugee protections have long been clear. These became increasingly apparent throughout the second half of the twentieth century as new types of conflicts and persecution took shape, especially as decolonization, the Cold War, diverse insurgencies, and new social movements reshaped the ways in which nations, nationalism, and identity were understood by institutions and individuals alike. For example, while the original treaty was focused on those who had been forced to cross an international border in order to be counted as a refugee, today the category of 'internally displaced persons' is a major sub-grouping recognized by the UNHCR. And while neither development nor environmental refugees are currently recognized internationally, a lively debate continues that they should be (Steiner, Gibney and Loescher, 2013; Gemenne, 2011).

The politics of refugee determination also has other geopolitical implications beyond who a given nation will extend protections to. Refugees have long been a part of Cold War politics – for example, much of US refugee policy between the end of the Second World War and the fall of the Soviet Union had mainly to do with US national interests and the government of the nation the migrant was fleeing and very little to do with the circumstances resulting in the flight (Hamlin and Wolgin 2012). But the politics of refugee determination extend far beyond just these definitional debates. Indeed, the shifting notions of 'refugee' and 'migrant' and how such terms are deployed and contested have at their core geopolitical questions as Allen et. al (2018) argue. For these authors the treatment of refugees and asylum seekers by nation-states and international institutes is not just about protection and sanctuary but more generally about the nature of citizenship, belonging and national identity:

> Being a migrant is embedded in national, geopolitical histories ... [migration] ... is not just about migrants, but is entangled with multiple policies, practices and processes that stretch across time, spaces and places (Allen et. al, 2018, 220).

In a similar vein, Hyndman (2012) has argued that geopolitics are central to understanding the ways that the mobilities and migrations of certain populations are always linked to particular historical identities and contexts. This is not, of course, a new phenomenon. In Ashutosh and Mountz's study of Chinese and Sri Lankan Tamil refugees in Canada (Ashutosh and Mountz 2012), the authors argue that geopolitical considerations structure every interaction between those seeking protection and those adjudicating their claims as well as all those encountering them throughout the process; they argue that "refugee flows are inherently geopolitical projects". They suggest moreover that when it comes to asylum cases, "the claimant process reproduces racist and colonial scripts between states, with the progressive and enlightened policies of receiving countries effectively obscuring their role in contributing to conflict and oppression" (Ashutosh and Mountz 2012, 340).

There are few elements of the contemporary global refugee regime where such connections are explicitly acknowledged. One example is the Special Immigrant Visa (SIV) program in the US, designed to approve the resettlement of Afghans and Iraqis who have worked as translators with US military or civil authorities in their own country and face persecution as a result (US Department of State 2019). But such initiatives have been a tiny part of a resettlement program that as previously described is already extremely limited in scope. Today, such programs that respond as diplomatic imperatives to the chaos caused by foreign political, economic and military interventions are less common. Instead, refugee policies are inextricably bound to national debates in countries of the Global North (and in some cases in entire regions) regarding immigration and demographic change.

Again, this is not a new phenomenon. The guest worker 'crises' of the 1960 s and 1970 s in Europe provoked similar anxieties. Indeed, by the early 1990 s and after the fall of the Soviet Union, much scholarship was devoted to the question of what immigration might look like in a post-Cold War world. Where earlier asylum policies had focused on the geopolitical interests of superpowers, different issues now came to the fore. In the US during this period the growing number of undocumented workers and stuttering attempts at immigration reform came to a head. In Europe the in-migration of people from former colonies over past decades had fundamentally changed the demographics and politics of many countries.

Many of the tensions we see in the contemporary moment thus have their roots in this long history, resulting in what Joppke (1998) described two decades ago as a clash between increasingly restrictionist domestic immigration politics and state infrastructures and policies committed to international rights, norms and treaties. As we entered a new millennium, he asked a question still relevant today: how is it possible that liberal democratic states with a vocal anti-immigrant polity may yet embrace an expansive immigration practice? Others have similarly asked how a so-called 'policy gap' might exist between those who seek to shut down immigration and those who wish to see it broadened (Cornelius, Martin and Hollifield 2004)? Freeman (1995, 882) has similarly argued that when looking at settler societies, post-imperial nations, and newer immigrant destination countries, "official policies tend to be more liberal than public opinion and annual intakes larger than is politically optimal." It is clear therefore that many writing in this period of increasing global integration had many questions about what the future might hold.

Twenty-five years later, it is apparent that such tensions have not been resolved. National interests remain firmly rooted in migration policies and have not been supplanted by internationalist ideals, whatever the suspicions of anti-globalist movements across the political spectrum might believe. In the US, Canada, and Australia ongoing debates centre on demographic shifts from being predominantly white settler colonial nations to ones that are more multicultural and racially/ethnically diverse. In the US in particular, the anxieties provoked by these changes find greatest embodiment in what Chavez (2013) has called the 'Latino threat narrative'; the presence of Latinx labour migrants in the US, of asylum seekers at the US Southern border, or simply the presence of Latinx bodies in the country at all. But others, especially refugees from Muslim-majority nations, have come to symbolize a related existential threat for many in the US – regarding religion, language, culture and politics. As Allen et. al. suggests "the very categories of migrants and refugees are changing in moments of crises ... [and] ... processes of categorization and governance have wider geopolitical implications for our understandings of nations, states and citizens (Allen et. al., 2018, 221).

Accepting or rejecting refugees therefore becomes not framed by humanitarian ideals or foreign policy goals that many actors involved in refugee work might invoke – protecting civilians or advancing peace in the Middle East for example – but rather what kind of nation a resettlement country might be after absorbing newcomers. In Europe, the rise of nativism and populism is especially noticeable following the influx of mainly Muslim migrants from Africa and the Middle East over recent decades. Formerly fringe far-right political parties and their xenophobic, racist rhetoric and policies have become part of the mainstream. Yet the anti-immigrant views they espouse have a longer history and influence on European (as well as global) border-making. What we might call a 'Muslim threat narrative' in Europe has resulted from national anxieties regarding demographic changes in many countries; the response to irregular migration has thus become increasingly securitized. Vollmer argues that "[most] migration control regimes were transformed – in the 1990 s but more intensively in the 'age of terrorism' – into securitization regimes" (Vollmer 2016, 720), while Hyndman suggests that "the securitization of migration, in particular, is a defining feature of current geopolitics" (Hyndman 2012, 243). Gilbert argues that

> Europe has treated refuge protection as part of its immigration policy: immigration law is about controlling entry, whereas refugee law should be about offering protection. This fusion of immigration and asylum, though, appears to be a fixture of refugee protection and one that will definitely continue to shape the development of the law in the future (Gilbert 2009, 57).

At its core, the European approach to refugees and asylum reveals a fundamentally ethnocentric view of regional identity, one in which borderless mobility was to be enjoyed by citizens of member states – but only by those seen as legitimate members of 'the club'. We see the national identity struggles that have ensued especially following the 2004 enlargement of the European Union to include a number of Central and Eastern European countries (Goodwin and Milazzo 2017). The influx of so many asylum seekers a decade later precipitated a similar set of struggles. In Vollmer's view "the 'refugee crisis' of 2014/2015 has shown in a most illustrative way how dysfunctional the EU migration regime is and how inappropriate the logic of bordering has become in the twenty-first century" (Vollmer 2016, 718).

Holmes and Castañeda (2016) suggest that the sense of crisis in the EU regarding refugees is not just about the influx of so many asylum seekers, but that the rise of anti-immigrant and anti-refugee discourse in countries like Germany and France is part of a broader political strategy adopted by Eurosceptic and populist parties across Europe to argue against the very project of the EU. Stockemer (2016) in his study of the vote gains by far-right political parties in Europe identifies negative perceptions of refugees, asylum-seekers and immigrants in general as core concerns for their supporters. Bauder links this trend to the increasing securitization of the European Union and its sense of territory and boundary:

> While freedom of migration was granted to people within the Schengen Area, Europe's external border hardened, making it increasingly difficult for people without prior authorization – including asylum seekers and refugees – to enter European territory. (Bauder 2016, 70)

The 'hardening' of the border has included not only reintroducing checkpoints and physical controls, but a literal and figurative extension of the borders of the EU. This has been done, for example, by signing agreements and providing incentives to governments in Turkey, Libya, Morocco and Tunisia to regulate migrant flows or to detain or warehouse refugees who might otherwise be heading for Europe (Bisong 2019).

Such policies have become all too common elsewhere. Watkins describes, for example, the ways that Australia has sought to stem the flow of migrants to its shores through investments of foreign aid and technical assistance to Syria, Afghanistan and other source countries to help control refugee outflows and in some cases encourage return migration:

> Australia has established an interconnected geography of border externalisations in source countries, countries of first asylum, and transit countries to make it more difficult for asylum seekers to cross borders (Watkins 2017, 965)

And such definitions can have drastic consequences, including the extension of detention regimes into (literally) extraterritorial regions, the ability to demonize and otherize forced migrants in multiple ways has led increasingly to the warehousing of refugees in carceral spaces across the globe. Braghiroli and Makarychev (2017) argue that Russia in particular has capitalized on these trends and has sought to actively foment discord regarding refugee policy within Europe as a way of re-entering continental politics. By supporting either tacitly or explicitly politicians and political groups that redefine Europe as anti-immigrant or illiberal in some other way, Russia in Braghiroli and Makarychev's view has weaponized refugee resettlement as a way to further its own aims. A similar retrenchment that continues to prioritize immigration rather than international agreements in refugee policy can also be seen in North America, with the case of Syrian refugees as an illustrative example.

Syrian Refugees and the Global Response

The exodus of so much of Syria's population is due to a number of factors including the civil war that has gripped the country since 2011. The country was severely destabilized by the US invasion of Iraq in 2003 and the subsequent rise of extremists in the region, especially the Islamic State group. Syria was also one of several countries caught up in the Arab Spring, a series of popular uprisings against military rule, oppressive regimes and dictatorships that led to the overthrow of governments in Egypt, Tunisia, and Libya and destabilized the region as a whole (Bayet 2017). In Syria, this uprising eventually morphed into a civil war, with the regime of Bashar al-Assad fighting initially against a number of secular and primarily Sunni Muslim rebel groups (Bakke and Kuypers 2016). Underlying tensions between various ethnic communities and both economic and environmental shocks contributed to further conflicts across Syria and the country was fractured by warring factions pursuing their own agendas.

Eventually a number of other countries and non-state actors were drawn into the conflict, with Iran and Shiite militias such as Hezbollah supporting Assad's forces, and the US and other western powers as well as the Gulf countries and Islamist forces including Al Qaeda and ISIS supporting (or indeed comprising) the various rebel factions (Bakke and Kuypers 2016). The entrance of Russia into the fray on the side of the Assad regime and the focus of the US and its allies on defeating ISIS in both Syria and Iraq decisively changed the conflict by 2016, moving into a new phase, and leaving a shattered country in its wake (Culcasi 2017; Okyay 2017). By 2018–2019 the conflict between Turkey and Syrian Kurds in the north of the country and the fall of the last rebel-held enclaves in other parts of Syria threatened to usher in yet more instability in the country, especially with the unexpected withdrawal by US President Trump of American forces from certain regions (Sly 2019).

It is not surprising that in light of all of this violence and sectarian conflict that many millions have fled their homes, seeing little hope for a peaceful resolution. Of Syria's pre-war population of nearly 22 million people, half have been displaced – an estimated six million internally and a further five million outside of the country, with yet another 2.5 million remaining in place but requiring humanitarian assistance (UNHCR, 2019). Of the overall total of Syrian forced migrants, a relatively small number actually been more permanently resettled in North American and Europe. Table 1 shows Syrians displaced as a result of the current conflict and the top 25 sites in which they currently reside:

Table 1. Syrians Displaced by the Civil War (UNHCR, 2019).

Country of Residence	Approximate Number of Displaced
Syria	6,600,000
Turkey	3,400,000
Lebanon	1,000,000
Jordan	660,000
Germany	530,000
Iraq	250,000
Egypt	130,000
Sweden	120,000
Yemen	100,000
Hungary	72,000
Canada	54,000
Croatia	55,000
Greece	55,000
Austria	50,000
US	33,000
Netherlands	32,000
Libya	27,000
Denmark	20,000
Belgium	17,000
Norway	14,000
Singapore	14,000
Switzerland	13,000
Serbia	12,000
France	11,500
UK	10,500

These figures clearly show that the response to this exodus has differed over time and by nation; there has been no unified response by the international community, as is not unusual in cases of forced migration, despite the existence of a global refugee regime. As in most cases of forced migration, those fleeing the conflict go to the closest safe haven – in most cases a neighbouring country. The countries most directly affected by the exodus were those in the immediate vicinity; indeed, while the numbers listed above are official figures from the UNHCR, many more have arrived through more informal channels, raising the numbers in Lebanon and Jordan to more than 2 million and 1 million Syrians seeking assistance respectively (Culcasi 2017). Key issues for such countries include an initial verification challenge to establish that those who arrive are in fact in legitimate need of protection, the capacity to house and provide support for so many non-citizens arriving with little means to provide for themselves, often for extended periods of time, and an effect on their own local communities and politics. In the case of Turkey, for example, the country has long struggled with calls for self-determination and rights amongst its Kurdish minority – the arrival of Syrian Kurds amongst the refugees and ethnic solidarities with Turkish Kurds added another dimension of complexity to the situation (Okyay 2017).

For many of the Syrian refugees the situation in neighbouring countries seemed equally tenuous as staying at home, and with little seeming resolution on the horizon, many fled further afield. This led to a large-scale migration across dangerous routes, both by land and sea, as increasing numbers sought asylum in other countries. By 2015, European countries were in the grip of a full scale 'crisis' – though the numbers of Syrians arriving in Europe were generally in the tens of thousands, not millions as in countries of the Middle East. The initial responses were primarily humanitarian in nature, as the world in general recoiled at the images of dead migrants – especially children – washing up on the shores of Italy and Greece (Doboš 2017). In Germany, over half a million Syrians were granted asylum, while the European Union agreed to take smaller numbers in other countries as well as to provide support to Turkey in exchange for lessening the flow of migrants through that country and into Europe (Ostrand 2015). Such measures – in combination with the evolution of the actual conflict in Syria – have helped to abate the exodus from the country. But as ISIS/ISIL lost its once vast territories in Iraq and Syria, new threats of instability continue with questions regarding the treatment of internally displaced, the threat of a guerilla war by the defeated parties in the conflict, the diverse motivations of external actors like the US, Russia, Turkey and Iran continue (O'Connor 2018). The threat of continued displacements both internally and externally from Syria remains high.

The prospect of accepting Syrians as refugees has, of course, become a deeply controversial debate in many parts of the world. It has resulted in a serious backlash against Syrians and Muslims in particular and against refugees in general within many western liberal democracies that have for several decades been the bedrock of the global resettlement system. This situation was not created as a result of the Syrian conflict – the backlash can instead be attributed to a number of factors. These include rising radicalization and terrorist attacks worldwide, increasing support for right wing political movements, xenophobia and Islamophobia in western countries, and various kinds of instability across the global system. Yet the Syrian crisis in many ways catalysed and intensified these existing debates and Syrian refugees became a symbol and a touchstone for important questions regarding immigration, humanitarian obligations, and national identity.

The US Response and Canadian Responses

In the United States the initial response to the crisis had been to accept Syrian refugees above and beyond existing resettlement quotas – the Obama administration had planned to accept an additional 10,000 Syrians in 2015 and nearly 30,000 in 2016 (Federal Register 2016). For the Obama administration, this was a question of both need – by 2015 there were over 45 million refugees and displaced persons worldwide – and of the US having the capacity to absorb more refugees. The US refugee program has long placed foreign policy objectives at its core (Haines, 2010); extending the capacity of the US Refugee Admissions Program (USRAP) by a few thousand or tens of thousands of Syrian refugees was thus a potential way of strengthening the US role as a mediator in the Middle East. The USRAP was already settling approximately 75,000 refugees per year during the last term of the Obama administration (RPC, 2019) and adding more resettlement sites was well in line with the US system's capacity (Federal Register 2016). Between 2015–2016, nearly 15,000 Syrians were resettled in the US (RPC, 2019), yet the backlash against Syrians in particular (and refugees in general) in the US intensified during the 2016 presidential campaign and continued on into the first years of the Trump administration, with repeated attempts to block Syrians entry into the country and successful caps on refugee admissions. Many governors and other politicians specifically sought to bar Syrians from resettling in their states.

What caused this backlash against Syrian refugees in the US? Some scholars have pointed to a similar growing trend of Islamophobia and anti-immigrant sentiment in the US as seen elsewhere in the world (Zunes 2017; Nagel, 2018 ; Ehrkamp). Trump and other politicians repeatedly raised concerns – with no evidence – regarding the screening and verification of Syrians and the supposed attempts by extremists to infiltrate migration routes (Rettberg and Gajjala 2016; Scribner 2017). Exacerbating latent xenophobia and engaging in racist dog-whistling has been a hallmark of politicians of this ilk – once in power, Trump has shown little sign of pivoting away from attacks on refugees and other immigrants and his administration has done everything in its power to limit arrivals, in addition to attacking other forms of legal and irregular migration (Pierce, Bolter, and Selee 2018).

Yet the initial response to the Syrian crisis in the US as elsewhere *was* different – there was an embrace of the refugees and a planned expansion of resettlement sites (Bose, 2018). The crucial turning point identified by many scholar and practitioners within the global refugee regime – from one of concern to one of fear – occurred in November 2015, with the mass killing of civilians in Paris by terrorists pledging allegiance to ISIS and explicitly referencing Syria (Nail 2016). The existing unease with the acceptance of large groups of refugees and asylum seekers intensified and the end of 2015 saw a significant shift in the discourse about and treatment of refugees worldwide (Savun and Ginesete, 2019). A growing number of terrorist attacks in cities in Europe and North America – many of them falsely blamed upon or associated with Syrian refugees – created a backlash against their acceptance in Europe and elsewhere (Pope 2017).

Refugee resettlement, which has always represented a fairly small part of the overall immigration landscape in the US, became increasingly politicized. Multiple state governors and a smaller number of cities announced in November 2015 (following the mass attacks in Paris) that they would no longer support refugee resettlement in their areas. The issue became a central feature of the Republican presidential primaries in 2015–2016, with Donald Trump taking a leading role in advocating against refugee resettlement, especially from Muslim-majority countries. In 2016 states like Texas and Maine officially withdrew from the USRAP, though refugees were still resettled in those states, especially Texas which has had the largest share of refugee arrivals in the US (Kennedy, 2016). More recently Texas announced that all resettlements would be banned. This is not surprising given the power that Trump has given to individual states and cities to exercise a veto power over refugee placements. The first years of the Trump presidency has ushered in an era of uncertainty and anxiety for the USRAP.

In one of his first acts, President Trump instituted a ban on arrivals from several Muslim majority nations as well as an immediate suspension and review of the USRAP, all in the name of national security. While these so-called 'travel bans' were challenged successfully in court in the years to follow, the resettlement program in particular was deeply affected (Pierce and Meissner, 2017). Where the USRAP and the many government and non-profit agencies that comprise, the program had planned on expanding in 2017, in practice what occurred was the opposite. The program ended up settling little more than 50,000 people – far less than half of what the Obama Administration had planned, and more in line with what the original travel ban had threatened. In 2018, the USRAP was approved to resettle just 45,000 people and in reality accepted just over 20,000(Federal Register 2017). In 2019 even fewer – 30,000 refugees – were approved for admittance into the US (Federal Register 2018). Syrians, as part of the overall travel ban eventually upheld by the Supreme Court, were barred with few exceptions from entering the country (Galbraith 2018). For 2020, the proposed number of refugee entrants dropped to even lower levels – a planned 18,000 as the upper ceiling of admitted arrivals (Federal Register 2019). With the onset of the COVID-19 pandemic and the resulting halt to most immigrant arrivals, just over 7,000 refugees in total are estimated to be resettled in the US in 2020.

A very different response to the Syrian crisis can be found to the US' neighbour to its north. Unlike the US – with which it has many geographic parallels in terms of proximity and social structure if not size – Canada has accepted a large number of Syrian refugees in a relatively short period of time. Canada's history of refugee resettlement has slightly older roots than that of the US, beginning in 1969 and from the outset more closely aligned with multilateral institutions such as the UN. The Canadian model included a private sponsorship component (as did its US counterpart initially) but is one that remains more fully state-directed than the USRAP (Voegeli 2014).

The resettlement program that has evolved in Canada has become an integral part of the global refugee regime. Like other third country resettlement sites within this system, Canadian acceptance rates have fluctuated over time largely in response to domestic and geopolitical interests (Ashutosh and Mountz 2012; Reynolds and Hyndman 2014). As a country that is roughly a tenth the size of the US in terms of population, Canada has traditionally resettled far fewer refugees than its neighbour in nominal terms but as a percentage of their overall populations both countries have accepted refugees at similar rates in recent decades. Indeed, since the end of the Cold War, the refugee recognition policies of the two countries have been more aligned than not, with similar groups being granted protection in each.

The integration of the two countries' resettlement and asylum determination systems can perhaps most clearly be seen in the Safe Third Country Agreement enacted by the two countries in 2004. This agreement, modelled after earlier so-called 'Fortress Europe' policies meant in that continent to limit the scope of asylum claims, ensures that those seeking protection in the US and Canada cannot travel through either country to register a claim in the other – a policy that mainly serves to decrease claims in Canada given the history of denial of Latin American claimants in the US and their subsequent journeys to Canada (Garcia 2006). One of the major differences between the Canadian and US resettlement systems is that the former is a primarily state-led program while the latter is a private-public partnership between the federal government and a number of non-profit resettlement agencies.

In terms of Syrian refugees, by 2019, Canada had accepted and resettled some 54,560 individuals. Canada had screened and selected potential new arrivals in partnership with the UNHCR. Of those who were approved, 26,240 arrived as Government-Assisted Refugees (GAR), 23,495 as Privately Sponsored Refugees (PSR), and a further 4,830 through a hybrid initiative known as the Blended Sponsorship Refugee (BSR) program (IRCC, 2019). While private sponsorships had previously been limited in the Canadian refugee system, the Syrian crisis meant a significant change to Canada's refugee policies, with private sponsors rather than government agencies helping to provide direct resettlement assistance including shelter, transportation and employment assistance . Whether arriving in Canada as government or privately sponsored refugees, Syrians were settled throughout the country and included a significant proportion of refugees under the age of 18. Unlike in the US, there was general public approval for the resettlement of Syrian refugees, an attitude that led to the reprioritization of private sponsorship as a mechanism.

As in the US case, Syrian refugees were an important part of a national election in Canada. Yet in Canada, the political party that made fear of Syrian refugees a central part of their party plank did not win. The incumbent government in the 2015 Canadian federal election, the Conservative Party of Canada, evoked familiar fears of the Muslim other, of Syrians as potential (or actual) terrorists, and sought to stoke cultural anxieties regarding demographic change – going so far as to create a tipline to solicit anonymous reports on Muslim neighbours (Gravelle 2018). The opposition Liberals were led by the Justin Trudeau, son of a former prime minister, who campaigned explicitly on accepting more Syrian refugees – and fulfilling this campaign promise upon winning election became the first priority of the new government.

Commonalities and Differences

Why was the response to the same crisis so different between Canada and the US? Canadian nationalists often argue that Canadian 'values' are reflected in this distinction – of a country that emphasizes a commitment to multiculturalism, multilateralism and tolerance (Wallace 2018). Certainly, much of Canadian identity has long been grounded in a negative definition – that it is "not the US" rather than "something Canadian". Yet it is a fiction that Canada is immune to the kind of rising Islamophobia, xenophobia and anti-immigrant and specifically anti-immigrant sentiments on display south of its borders. One needs only look at the killings of worshippers in a mosque in Quebec in 2017 (Mahrouse 2018) or the explicitly anti-refugee platforms of various political parties – including the successful 2018 campaign of the Progressive Conservatives in Ontario (Silver, Taylor, and Calderón-Figueroa 2020) – and the rise in hate crimes against Muslims and refugees to see evidence of this (Elkassem et al.; Perry 2015). And scholars such as Dauvergne has examined the actual outcomes of asylum cases in Canada to question its real commitment to refugee protections:

> There are a good many reasons to think that Canada is likely to be as good as it gets for noncitizen access to international human rights. If that is right, the results are a dismal showing indeed (Dauvergne 326)

In this final section of the paper, I draw on interviews with resettlement officials in both countries to understand the different approaches to the Syrian refugee crisis. Ashutosh and Mountz (2012) and Torres (2018) suggest that understanding the dynamics of geopolitical relations requires not only an analysis of structural conditions at the macro level but equally an examination of the embodied meanings, discourses and practices of actors at the micro scale. Other scholars have similarly argued that focusing on the agents of the state rather than institutional structures allows us to decode and deconstruct how immigration practice comes into being, and how policies may be enacted, resisted, and transformed (Prince 2013). Does there indeed exist a 'policy gap' between the general public and state policy when it comes to refugees and if so, is it seen or articulated by key actors? Is there a distinction between what Hammar described as 'immigration policy' (which governs the integration or experiences of those admitted to nation-states) and 'immigration control' (which governs those who are admitted in the first place)? Do Canada and the US remain fundamentally liberal democratic states whose embrace of international protection norms overcome restrictionist impulses?

Between 2014 and 2018 the author conducted a series of interviews with key informants involved with resettlement in Canada and the US to explore such questions. This was part of a broader project looking at refugee resettlement in North America and Europe during this period. The interviews on which this analysis is based consisted of a sub-set of forty individuals, twenty in each country, including governmental and non-governmental officials at the federal, state/provincial, and municipal levels. Because of the sensitive nature of the topic, interviewees asked not to be identified by name but rather by a description of their role.

There were several common themes that became clear through the course of these interviews. I will focus on three particular ones in the remainder of this section: 1) the desirability of certain kinds of refugees, b) the rise of xenophobic rhetoric in official discourse and practice, and c) a sense of fatigue regarding the official policy of each of the governments in power in 2015–2016 towards Syrian refugees. Taken together, these statements by key informants in Canadian and US resettlement suggest that these domestic election concerns rather than international political priorities played a defining role in the different outcomes and that as a result the 'gap' between politics and policy may be less significant than previously theorized.

The Desirability of Syrian Refugees

One of the questions I asked interviewees about had to do with plans for accepting Syrians in the US pre- and post-2016. This was not simply about the logistics of resettlement but rather the logic of acceptance, since selection of those deemed worthy to be admitted has always played an important role, especially in the US system. If Cold War considerations once drove US refugee policy and a post-Cold War adherence to emerging international norms characterized the most recent period, how might the response to the Syria crisis be understood? A former State Department official told me:

> Originally, we assumed we would get no Syrian refugees anyway. Everyone was saying back in 2013 that there'd be none left – the Italians or the French would snap them all up, they'd want them because they were well-educated, spoke English, came from big cities, and would have all kinds of skills. After the election campaign and then Trump that changed in a big hurry.

What this official articulates is a kind of enlightened self-interest which has at its core a benefit to the receiving country. The refugees here are desirable because they bring skills, are apparently urban, and speak English; in other words, the supports needed for acculturation would be limited. The emphasis here is on how the Syrians might act upon arrival, not the legitimacy of their claim to protection. Ironically, such a view aligns well with the kinds of changes that the Trump administration has sought to make to legal immigration since taking office, drastically curtailing certain flows (including refugees, asylums seekers and family reunification) and putting an emphasis on skilled migration.

Another resettlement agency director in the US also speaks of Syrians in terms of their desirability, yet here the focus is on protection – at least initially:

> In 2015 it was all we could do to keep up with all the requests to resettle Syrian refugees. We'd get calls from a church group in Arkansas or a community organization in Nebraska or some faith-based community in Ohio or someone else who'd seen the pictures of Alan Kurdi and wanted to know what they could do. Then the election happened and ... well ... you know ...

The sentiment referenced here is a humanitarian impulse articulated by segments of the general public to help those who have been harmed. The desirability of Syrians here rests on the legitimacy of their claim to protection. An official with one of the provincial partner agencies in Canada referenced a similar enthusiasm for resettling Syrians:

> Honestly, sometimes it could get a bit much. I'd get calls from this mayor or that councilor or this family asking when were they getting the Syrians. It's like they all wanted their own Syrian doll family.

Another individual with IRCC voiced a similar kind of frustration:

> I mean it's great that people want to help. But there are more than just Syrian refugees out there and it became difficult to get people to want to help Congolese refugees or other groups in need of protection. This was especially hard because the Liberal Government made Syrians such an important symbol, especially during the campaign.

Each of these officials gives voice to the idea that Syrians were – at least initially – seen as 'good' or 'deserving' refugees. They also speak to a balance that these officials seem to recognize at least implicitly between official policies and mechanisms on the one hand and public sentiment and politics on the other. Public enthusiasm for sponsoring more refugees, opening new resettlement sites and wanting specific refugee groups can be contrasted here with international obligations and the realities of resettlement. Of course, public sentiment was by no means wholly or even substantially in support of refugees, as the following theme demonstrates.

The Rise of Xenophobic Rhetoric

Key respondents within the refugee regimes I interviewed returned again and again to the theme that they found themselves surrounded by increasing levels of vitriol and suspicion of refugees – not amongst fringe anti-immigrant movements, but at the highest levels of their own governments and by officials even within the resettlement apparatus in each country. Such a dynamic calls into question whether there does indeed exist a 'policy gap' between the bureaucratic immigration infrastructure of liberal democratic states and the xenophobia of segments of its polity – or whether instead the ascendancy of particular politics allows a particular viewpoint to flourish, whether expansionist or restrictionist.

For both sets of interviewees, the intensification of of a xenophobic rhetoric was especially apparent during the 2015 and 2016 election campaigns. One IRCC official stated:

> Oh my god that tip line – that tip line! [rolls eyes] What was the government thinking? I can't begin to tell you how stupid and flat out racist some of the tips we got were. It was like encouraging everyone's worst instincts.

The respondent here references a phone hotline that the Canadian federal government proposed to essentially call out aberrant or dangerous behaviour by immigrants. Critics called out the Islamophobic and racist assumptions embedded in such an initiative, directed as it was at the ongoing moral panics regarding Islamic extremism in the Global North.

Another provincial resettlement official had this to say about the public and private responses to Syrian resettlement in Canada:

> I would say that as a whole they were accepted across the country. Whether each and every individual has the same understanding or acceptance level, it's a broad base question that's very difficult to answer. I will say that it's not all milk and honey. There's a lot of places where there's a lot of backlash in the background but because we're Canadian we're too polite to say it out loud.

In both of the preceding quotes there is a distance between the resettlement official and both the politicians and the public that they serve. The tip line is not (only) a bad idea for being racist and a political failure, it will encourage 'the worst instincts' in the general public. The backlash against resettlement is impolite (or un-Canadian) to articulate aloud, yet the second respondent makes it clear that it is all too present.

But the xenophobia was not only from without. Another IRCC official spoke of the rising tensions within their own agency as the political campaign heated up:

> I felt there was a huge level of scrutiny even though we're all civil servants and supposed to remain professional and above politics. Did we say anything too pro-refugee? Did we seem like we're favoring one group or set of policies? I felt like we just had to keep our heads down and stay out of the spotlight but it was pretty hard to do.

One might well ask whether civil servants could ever occupy the neutral, mediating space articulated by this respondent – certainly as Ashutosh and Mountz (2012) point out, the interaction that refugees and asylum seekers have with such figures are anything but dispassionate. The effect of politics – not just policy – within resettlement agencies and bureaucracies are, therefore central to our understanding of how shifts may occur.

In the US, a former official in the Office of Refugee Resettlement said that the rise to prominence of anti-refugee sentiments and views took many in their agency by surprise:

> This is not the first or last time that refugees will be controversial, I know. These things go in cycles. But honestly, this program has always had lots of support, from across the aisle. How could we predict that all of a sudden we would be the ones in the crosshairs, told we were the reason for a security threat, that shutting us down was necessary?

The scrutiny and the spotlight here are both from the general public and the politicians that the resettlement officials putatively work for. One might well ask, however, how this respondent had been unable to predict the backlash – having worked within the resettlement apparatus had they been insulated from the rising tensions regarding immigration? Had the history of bipartisan support for the USRAP made the respondent feel they could ignore or avoid the controversy rising around them?

Another respondent, an official currently in the US government involved with refugee resettlement bemoaned the discourse increasingly adopted by segments of the general population:

> I wish people actually knew something about refugees. Instead they just watch whatever show that scares them, they hear Trump go out and tell them how little he knows and then they worry about who's coming to their hometown. So, no surprise they're going to go and vote for the guy who tells them he'll keep the scary terrorists away.

Another resettlement official at the state level in the US complained:

> The presidential campaign was the worst. Every time Trump (or one of the others) came through, I'd get a bunch of phone calls from mayors all of a sudden freaked out about who we placed in their city. Or from people asking us questions about Sharia law and things like that.

The overall impression one gets from the preceding quotes is that these officials – all involved with the plans to resettle Syrians in Canada and the US in 2015-2016 – view themselves as professional civil servants defending humanitarian norms against a rising tide of xenophobia and ignorance in each of their countries. Yet as the literature previously reviewed reminds us, this is not the first time we have seen a backlash against immigration or even refugees, whether in these two countries or in other parts of the Global North. But perhaps the role of these agents of the state has been overestimated – perhaps there is less of a policy gap between politics and the implementation of immigration control than has been posited. If Canada had re-elected the Harper government, which had run its campaign on relatively anti-immigrant grounds, would Syrians have been resettled in such numbers? The answer would seem to be no, especially given the number of anti-immigrant campaigns run by political parties in the years since the Syrian resettlement at both the federal and provincial levels, and by the adoption of anti-immigrant legislation in Quebec and Ontario.

2015/2016 and Anti-Government Backlash

An interesting dynamic that key informants in both countries mentioned was the sense that they witnessed a backlash against the refugee policies of previous regimes. In the US these were directed at the Obama administration and specifically the plans to increase Syrian resettlement as mentioned by this federal resettlement official:

> When we started the R&P [reception and placement] consultations even as early as FY2016, oh my god the amount of pushback about even the idea of Syrians. A lot of it started out with questions about process and transparency but pretty soon you'd end up being forced to answer why Obama wants Sharia law in Iowa or Ohio or something like that.

A state level resettlement official similarly reported that local discussions regarding Syrian resettlement in the US were being overtaken by the national discourse, especially animated by groups opposed to and organized against refugee resettlement such as Refugee Resettlement Watch and its leader Ann Corcoran:

> We spent a lot of time and effort trying to plan for good outcomes, working with local partners and organizations. We felt like we had a really good plan to present to the city council and the general public. We had real local support, grassroots groups that were out there fundraising and preparing and excited to welcome Syrian families. Next thing we know Ann Corcoran's breezed into town and whipped up all this anti-immigrant, anti-refugee craziness, saying it's all part of Obama's plan to destroy America and that real Americans need to resist it.

In both of the preceding quotes, a distrust of the Obama administration – and Obama himself – motivates part of the backlash, especially amongst a certain, mainly right-wing segment of the population. And as in the response to xenophobic rhetoric, there is a sense of dismissiveness in the tone of the respondents. But as another official with a federal agency lamented:

> We lost control of the narrative a very long time ago. I would say when we VOLAGs [Voluntary Agencies] became professionalized. Lots of refugees used to say we're too much like the government, all we care about is numbers, not what really happens to them. So when all these people started criticizing us and all these nutjobs started attacking us on talk shows and in the media, who was going to stand up for us? We started to get organized with actual refugee communities, but that was a long time later. By that time it was way too late and all the political appointees were already telling us to tear it all down.

The apparatus of the refugee regime in the US is shown to be more fragile and susceptible to change based on political leaders than we might have imagined

In Canada too there was a backlash in 2015 against current government policy on refugees – but it was in the opposite direction as that in the US. When I asked one official in Canada regarding the particular dynamic that saw so much of the electorate apparently embrace Trudeau's pro-refugee message, she responded:

> I think people were just tired of so many years of Harper. They wanted to prove that we're a better people than that, that we're willing to help. I don't know how much they really understand refugees, but they wanted to show that they're not like that. And that hotline was just a terrible idea.

Another interviewee who works at the municipal level with refugees echoed this sentiment:

> I can't tell you that people actually really love refugees but I can tell you they like to think that they're a people who really love refugees. And the Harper government made it easy to pick a side – if you're the two-thirds or so of the country that doesn't vote for the Conservatives, it's an easy way to show you're not down with demonizing them and that you're for immigration and being a peacekeeper country and all that.

Yet another provincial resettlement official illustrated this dynamic with the following story:

> I was in two city hall meetings about six months apart, pretty small town by my standards and you had this, you know, kind of growing sentiment where they said "We want Syrians, we want to show welcome, we want to show that, you know ... in my words, Harper's candidate doesn't define who we are. There's a global crisis and we're going to meet it."

In these interviews with stakeholders in the refugee regimes in both countries, the importance of Syrian refugees as symbols of each country's attitude and approach towards refugees and immigrants was clear. In the 2015 Canadian election, the Liberal party placed acceptance of Syrians front and centre, and upon its victory, the Trudeau government went about facilitating the resettlement of significant numbers. In the 2016 US Presidential election, Donald Trump (and most other Republican candidates) made the rejection of Syrian refugees an explicit goal of his campaign. In the preceding interviews, the perspectives of key informants intimately involved with resettlement in each country give compelling insights into what ultimately drove differing responses to the Syrian refugee crisis. We thus see in these two cases the ways in which domestic political priorities – rather than explicitly geopolitical goals – can have a profound impact on central players in the global refugee regime.

Conclusion

When we look at the dynamics of Syrian refugee resettlement in Canada and the US since 2015, the broader issue of the fragility of the global refugee regime to local contexts and politics becomes clearer. The insights provided by key informants in the preceding section makes apparent that some of the most important factors in determining acceptance or rejection of Syrians had more to do with domestic immigration politics – how sympathetically the general public viewed a potential refugee population, how prevalent xenophobic or anti-immigrant sentiments had become, and how the electorate viewed the contemporary government's refugee policies – than with international humanitarian obligations. The long-term impact of these particular political moments and dynamics – a civil war in Syria coupled with national elections in Canada and the US – therefore cannot be understated.

Trudeau to many of his supporters represented a rejection of nine years of Conservative rule under Stephen Harper, years in which refugee and asylum protection had been severely curtailed. Trump, on the other hand, represented the opposite to many of his voters, a rejection of the supposedly 'globalist' and 'progressive' agenda that embrace refugees. Both of these characterizations are of course deeply reductive, and yet they speak to the motivations of at least a sizable group of voters who supported Trudeau and Trump respectively.

Yet what do such dynamics have to tell us about the current and perhaps future state of the global refugee protection systems? On the one hand there is abundant evidence that national interests have always dominated migration policies; in this sense the 2015 Canadian and 2016 US federal elections and their respective environments do not represent a new moment in international relations or the global refugee regime. And yet the voices of key figures within both sets of domestic refugee apparatuses that I interviewed suggest a clear sense of rupture, that *something* is indeed changing in the

global refugee and protection systems as we know them. The progressive closing down of the USRAP and the targeting of Syrian refugees in particular as emblematic of security and social risks has had a ripple effect throughout the global refugee regime, with many countries already under pressure from right wing, populist and especially xenophobic movement both within and across borders. The willingness of the Trump administration to turn its back on longstanding commitments and multilateral processes in refugee determination and acceptance makes it easier for other countries to do the same. The progressive denial of asylum or refugee status to Syrians has often become a central theme in the political platforms of electoral candidates in the US and other European countries. These platforms are part of a broader trend of rising anti-immigrant discourse in many Western countries (Postelnicescu, 2016). It may be true that refugee policies have always been dictated by national interests, yet in concrete terms the last five years have seen a profound and measurable lessening of refugee protections worldwide.

Of course it may also be true that national interests may result in an outcome in the opposite direction. In a departure from many other Western countries, however, it was the *acceptance* of Syrian refugees that was associated with the electoral promises made by the governing Liberal Party of Canada in the 2015 federal election. There was in fact significant popular support for this initiative, as evidenced by the high participation rate of the general public in the private sponsorship program described previously (CJPME, 2015). Such support however did not prevent refugee policies from coming under attack in the most recent Canadian election in 2019, with the Trudeau government receiving its share of backlash over resettlement efforts (Llana 2019).

The broader issue is not, of course, how or whether Canada or the US response to the Syrian crisis is better, morally superior, or more effective. The larger question that should concern refugee advocates, communities and those concerned with international human rights and the rights of vulnerable populations is how we provide adequate global protections in a system that is as dependent on national and domestic political priorities as the current global refugee regime seems to be. In a world where xenophobia and anti-immigrant populism is on the rise and illiberalism threatens the very idea of multilateralism and efforts like the Global Compact on Migration, how do we hold nation-states and powerful actors accountable to sustainable and reliable commitments?

Acknowledgements

The author would like to thank Orhon Myadar, Kara Dempsey, Nancy Hiemstra as well as the anonymous reviewers for their valuable feedback throughout the preparation of this article.

Funding

This work was supported by the US National Science Foundation, Directorate for Social, Behavioral and Economic Sciences [1359895].

References

Allen, W., B. Anderson, N. Van Hear, M. Sumption, F. Düvell, J. Hough, L. Rose, R. Humphris, and S. Walker. 2018. Who counts in crises? The new geopolitics of international migration and refugee governance. *Geopolitics* 23 (1):217–43. doi:10.1080/14650045.2017.1327740.

Ashutosh, I., and A. Mountz. 2012. The geopolitics of migrant mobility: Tracing state relations through refugee claims, boats, and discourses. *Geopolitics* 17 (2):335–54. doi:10.1080/14650045.2011.567315.

Bakke, P. C., and J. A. Kuypers. 2016. The Syrian civil war, international outreach, and a clash of worldviews. *KB Journal* 11 (2):1–3.

Bauder, H. 2016. Understanding Europe's refugee crisis: A dialectical approach. *Geopolitics, History and International Relations* 8 (2):64–75.

Bayet, A. 2017. *Revolution without revolutionaries: Making sense of the Arab Spring*. Stanford: Stanford University Press.

Betts, A. and Loescher, G. (Eds) 2011. *Refugees in International Relations*. Oxford: Oxford University Press.

Bisong, A. 2019. Trans-regional institutional cooperation as multilevel governance: ECOWAS migration policy and the EU. *Journal of Ethnic and Migration Studies* 45 (8):1294–309. doi:10.1080/1369183X.2018.1441607.

Bose, P.S., 2018. Welcome and hope, fear, and loathing: The politics of refugee resettlement in Vermont. Peace and Conflict: Journal of Peace Psychology, 24(3): 320-329. doi:10.1037/pac0000302

Bradley, M. 2014. Rethinking refugeehood: Statelessness, repatriation and refugee agency. *Review of International Studies* 2014 (40):101–23. doi:10.1017/S0260210512000514.

Braghiroli, S., and A. Makarychev. 2017. Redefining Europe: Russia and the 2015 refugee crisis. *Geopolitics* 23 (4):823–48. doi:10.1080/14650045.2017.1389721.

Chavez, L. 2013. *The Latino threat: Constructing immigrants, citizens and the nation*. 2nd ed. Stanford: Stanford University Press.

CJPME. 2015. 2015 Election Guide - Syrian Refugee Crisis. Canadians for Justice and Peace in the Middle East. Last modified April 15, 2015. Accessed June 24, 2020. https://www.cjpme.org/an_2015_10_15_election_guide_syrian_refugees_crisis

Cornelius, Martin, Tsuda and Hollifield 2004 and add reference Cornelius, W., Martin, P., Tsuda, T., and Hollifield, J. (Eds) 2004. Controlling immigration: a global perspective. Stanford: Stanford University Press

Culcasi, K. 2017. Displacing territory: Refugees in the Middle East. *International Journal of Middle East Studies* 49 (2):323–26. doi:10.1017/S0020743817000095.

Devictor, X. and Do, Q-T. 2017. How manyyears have refugees been in exile? Population and Development Review. 43(2): 355–369. https://doi.org/10.1111/padr.12061

Doboš, P. 2017. Imaginative geographies of distant suffering: Two cases of the Syrian Civil War on television. *Social & Cultural Geography* 19 (6):764-788.

Ehrkamp, P. Geographies of migration II: the racial-spatial politics of immigration. *Progress in Human Geography*. 43(2): 363-375.

Elkassem, S., R. Csiernik, A. Mantulak, G. Kayssi, Y. Hussain, K. Lambert, P. Bailey, and A. Choudhary. 2018. Growing up Muslim: The impact of islamophobia on children in a Canadian community. *Journal of Muslim Mental Health* 12(1):3–18.

Federal Register. 2016. Presidential determination on refugee admissions for fiscal year 2017. 81 FR 70315. Executive office of the President. No. 2016-13. September 28

Federal Register. 2018. Presidential determination on refugee admissions for fiscal year 2019. 83 FR 55091. Executive office of the President. No. 2018-24135. October 4.

Federal Register. 2019. Presidential determination on refugee admissions for fiscal year 2020. 83 FR 55091. Executive office of the President. No. 2018-24135. November 1.

Freeman, G. P. 1995. Modes of immigration politics in liberal democratic states. *International Migration Review* 29 (4):881–902. doi:10.1177/019791839502900401.

Galbraith, J. 2018. US supreme court upholds presidential proclamation restricting entry of individuals from covered countries. *American Journal of International Law* 112 (4):741–45.

Garcia, M. C. 2006. Canada: A northern refuge for Central Americans. Migration Policy Institute. Last modified April 1, 2006. Accessed March 25, 2019. https://www.migrationpolicy.org/article/canada-northern-refuge-central-americans

Gemenne, F. 2011. Migrations and Population Displacements in a World at+ 4° C. Etudes 414 (6): 727–738

Gilbert, G. 2009. Spread too thin? The UNHCR and the new geopolitics of refugees. *Harvard International Review* 2009:56–59.

Goodwin, M., and C. Milazzo. 2017. Taking back control? Investigating the role of immigration in the 2016 vote for Brexit. *The British Journal of Politics and International Relations* 19 (3):450–64. doi:10.1177/1369148117710799.

Government of Canada. 2017. #WelcomeRefugees: Key Figures. Last modified February 27, 2017. Accessed March 25, 2019. https://www.canada.ca/en/immigration-refugees-citizenship/services/refugees/welcome-syrian-refugees/key-figures.html

Gravelle, T. 2018. Friends, neighbours, townspeople and parties: Explaining Canadian attitudes toward Muslims. *Canadian Journal of Political Science* 51 (3):643–64. doi:10.1017/S0008423917001470.

Hamlin, R., and P. Wolgin. 2012. Symbolic politics and policy feedback: The United Nations Protocol relating to the status of refugees and American refugee policy in the Cold War. *International Migration Review* 46 (3):586–624. doi:10.1111/j.1747-7379.2012.00898.x.

Holmes, S., and H. Castañeda. 2016. Representing the 'European refugee crisis' in Germany and beyond: Deservingness and difference, life and death. *American Ethnologist* 43 (1):12. doi:10.1111/amet.12259.

Hyndman, J. 2012. The Geopolitics of migration and mobility. *Geopolitics* 17 (2):243–55. doi:10.1080/14650045.2011.569321.

IRCC, 2019. Syrian Refugees - IRCC Monthly Updates. Last modified April 18, 2019. Accessed June 25, 2020. https://open.canada.ca/data/en/dataset/01c85d28-2a81-4295-9c06-4af792a7c209

Joppke, C. 1998. Why liberal states accept unwanted immigration. *World Politics* 50 (2):266–93. doi:10.1017/S004388710000811X.

Kennedy, M. Texas pulls out of federal refugee resettlement program. NPR. Last modified September 30, 2016. Accessed June 25, 2020. https://www.npr.org/sections/thetwo-way/2016/09/30/496098507/texas-pulls-out-of-federalrefugee-resettlement-program

Llana, S. 2019. Why Canada has cooled on Justin Trudeau. Last modifiedOctober162019. AccessedNovember 15, 2019. https://www.csmonitor.com/World/Americas/2019/1018/Why-Canada-has-cooled-on-Justin-Trudeau

Mahrouse, G. 2018. Minimizing and denying racial violence: Insights from the Québec mosque shooting. *Canadian Journal of Women and the Law* 30 (3):471–93. doi:10.3138/cjwl.30.3.006.

Nagel, C. 2018. Southern hospitality? Islamophobia and the politicization of refugees in South Carolina during the 2016 election season. *Southeastern Geographer* 56 (3):283–90. doi:10.1353/sgo.2016.0033.

Nail, T. 2016. A tale of two crises: Migration and terrorism after the Paris attacks. *Studies in Ethnicity and Nationalism* 16 (1):158–67. doi:10.1111/sena.12168.

O'Connor, T. 2018. Turkey is launching the next Middle East war with attacks on Kurds in Iraq and Syria. *Newsweek*. Last modified March 21, 2018. Accessed 2019 March 31, . https://www.newsweek.com/turkey-launching-nextmiddle-east-war-attacks-kurds-iraq-syria-855945

OCHA. 2019. Rohingya refugee crisis. United Nations Office for the coordination of humanitarian affairs. Last modified August 29, 2018. Accessed March 25, 2019. https://www.unocha.org/rohingya-refugee-crisis

Okyay, A. S. 2017. Turkey's post-2011 approach to its Syrian border and its implications for domestic politics. *International Affairs* 93 (4):829–46. doi:10.1093/ia/iix068.

Ostrand, N. 2015. The Syrian refugee crisis: A comparison of responses by Germany, Sweden, the United Kingdom, and the United States. *Journal on Migration and Human Security* 3 (3):255–79. doi:10.1177/233150241500300301.

Penz, P., J. Drydyk, and P. Bose. 2011. *Displacement by development: Ethics, rights and responsibilities*. Cambridge: Cambridge University Press.

Perry, B. 2015. 'All of a sudden, there are Muslims': Visibilities and Islamophobic violence in Canada. *International Journal for Crime, Justice and Social Democracy* 4 (3):4–15. doi:10.5204/ijcjsd.v4i3.235.

Pierce, S., J. Bolter, and A. Selee. 2018. US immigration policy under Trump: Deep changes and lasting impacts. *Migration Policy Institute*. Last modified July 2018. Accessed March 31, 2019. https://www.migrationpolicy.org/research/us-immigration-policy-trump-deep-changes-impacts

Pierce, S. and Meisner, D. 2017. Trump Executive Order on Refugees and Travel Ban: A Brief Review. Migration Policy Institute. Last modified February 2017. Accessed June 25, 2020. https://www.migrationpolicy.org/research/trump-executiveorder-refugees-and-travel-ban-brief-review

Pope, P. J. 2017. Constructing the refugee as villain: An analysis of Syrian refugee policy narratives used to justify a state of exception. *World Affairs* 180 (3):53–71. doi:10.1177/0043820018757542.

Postelnicescu, C. 2016. "Europe's new identity: The refugee crisis and the rise of nationalism", in Europe's Journal Of Psychology 12 (2): 203-209 doi:10.5964/ejop.v12i2.1191

Prince, R. 2013. Disaggregating the state: Exploring interdisciplinary possibilities for the study of policy. *Political Geography* 34 (2013):60–62. doi:10.1016/j.polgeo.2013.02.002.

Register, F. 2017. Presidential determination on refugee admissions for fiscal year 2018. 82 FR 49083. Executive office of the President. No. 2017-23140. September 29, 2017.

Rettberg, J. W., and R. Gajjala. 2016. Terrorists or cowards: Negative portrayals of male Syrian refugees in social media. *Feminist Media Studies* 16 (1):178–81. doi:10.1080/14680777.2016.1120493.

Reynolds, J., and J. Hyndman. 2014. A turn in Canadian refugee policy and practice. *Whitehead Journal of Diplomacy & International Relations* 16 (2):41–55.

Savun, B. and Gineste, C. 2019. From protection to persecution: Threat environment and refugee scapegoating. Journal of Peace Research, 56(1): 88-102. doi:10.1177/0022343318811432

Scribner, T. 2017. You are not welcome here anymore: Restoring support for refugee resettlement in the age of Trump. *Journal on Migration and Human Security* 5 (2):263–84. doi:10.1177/233150241700500203.

Silver, D., Taylor, Z. and Calderón-Figueroa, F. 2020. Populism in the City: the Case of Ford Nation, International Journal of Politics, Culture, and Society 33(1): 1-21. doi:10.1007/s10767-018-9310-1

Sly, K. 2019. Withdrawing US troops from Syria is proving easier said than done. *Washington Post*. Last modified February 8, 2019. Accesssed March 31, 2019. https://www.washingtonpost.com/world/withdrawing-us-troops-from-syria-is-proving-easier-said-than-done/2019/02/08/22092d22-249e-11e9-b5b4-1d18dfb7b084_story.html?noredirect=on&utm_term=.b07b8eb8de7e

Steiner, N., Gibney, M., and Loescher, G. (Eds) 2013. Problems of protection: The UNHCR, refugees and human rights. New York: Routledge.

Stockemer, D. 2016. Structural data on immigration or immigration perceptions? What accounts for the electoral success of the radical right in Europe? *JCMS: Journal of Common Market Studies* 54 (4):999–1016. doi:10.1111/jcms.12341.

Torres, R. 2018. A crisis of rights and responsibility: Feminist geopolitical perspectives on Latin American refugees and migrants. *Gender, Place and Culture* 25 (1):13–36. doi:10.1080/0966369X.2017.1414036.

Ullah, A. A., and S. Roy Choudhury. 2018. Geopolitics of conflicts and refugees in the Middle East and North Africa. *Contemporary Review of the Middle East* 5 (3):258–74. doi:10.1177/2347798918776751.

UNHCR. 2020. Figures at a Glance. Last modified June 18, 2020. Accessed June 24, 2020. https://www.unhcr.org/ph/figures-at-a-glance

US Department of State. 2019. Special immigrant visas (SIVs) for Iraqi and Afghan translators/interpreters. Accessed October 22, 2019. https://travel.state.gov/content/travel/en/us-visas/immigrate/siv-iraqi-afghan-translators-interpreters.html

Voegeli, S. 2014. Canadian sponsorship of refugees program reform: A limit of Canadians' generosity. Thesis. *University of Ottawa*, June, 2014.

Vollmer, B. 2016. New narratives from the EU external border – Humane refoulement? *Geopolitics* 21 (3):717–41. doi:10.1080/14650045.2016.1154843.

Wallace, R. 2018. Contextualizing the crisis: The framing of Syrian refugees in Canadian print media. *Canadian Journal of Political Science* 51 (2):207–31. doi:10.1017/S0008423917001482.

Watkins, J. 2017. Bordering borderscapes: Australia's use of humanitarian aid and border security support to immobilize asylum seekers. *Geopolitics* 22 (4):958–83. doi:10.1080/14650045.2017.1312350.

Zunes, S. 2017. Europe's refugee crisis, terrorism, and Islamophobia. *Peace Review* 29 (1):1–6. doi:10.1080/10402659.2017.1272275.

Migrant Agency and Counter-Hegemonic Efforts Among Asylum Seekers in the Netherlands in Response to Geopolitical Control and Exclusion

Kara E. Dempsey

ABSTRACT
Migrants who reach EU asylum camps face various forms of spatialised violence that are bolstered by or produced within these geopolitical protracted spaces of waiting. Segregated from society, migrants experience processes of displacement, alienation and vulnerability as their legal status restricts their mobility and postpones employment or education opportunities. They are simultaneously suspended in a state of continuous disruption as they move through a series of camps while waiting for a decision on their applications. In remonstration, some migrants develop advocacy networks within and across camps in an attempt to challenge the hierarchical control of the everyday spaces and politics that migrants encounter in camps. Drawing on original fieldwork, this paper interrogates the intersection of the spatial production of geopolitical violence in camps and migrant agency within these distinctive political spaces. I argue that a state-centred examination of spaces of violence and migrant agency fails to attend to embodied and emotional landscapes when problematising the geographies of camps and those waiting in interim zones of confinement. In contrast, this examination of the embodied migrant experiences and advocacy networks brings the geopolitics of human and affective matter to the forefront. In this way, the article highlights migrant agency in response to their lived experience and the embodied geopolitical violence of control, categorisation and exclusion that is produced in the various spatialities of asylum seeking.

Introduction

Life in this asylum camp is full of constant change and the unknown. It's a life under surveillance and full of wasted time. Since conditions here are not good, we have come together to advocate for improvements in the camp and more control over our lives while we wait (personal interview #8, spokesperson[1] for Asylum Seekers Alliance of Keipelgevangenis Camp, 2016).

An unpresented number of asylum seekers arrived in the Netherlands beginning in 2014 as part of a larger migration into Europe. Many experienced various forms of spatialised control and geopolitical violence produced by migration legislation (e.g., Casas-Cortes 2015; Dempsey 2018, 2020; Jones and Johnson 2016; Mitchell 2006; Mountz 2011). Throughout the application process, migrants reside in asylum camps that are often segregated from society. The camps are in effect geopolitical and temporal spaces of state control and generate forms of geopolitical violence via processes of exclusion, displacement, alienation and vulnerability for migrants. The quotation above from a Syrian asylum seeker and advocacy organiser illuminates the precarious conditions in which migrants remain trapped for an extended time. Bureaucratic processes pertaining to asylum applications in the Netherlands take extended periods of time, during which many migrants feel confused, fearful and forgotten as they spend months or years waiting for a decision on asylum – what many consider a form of abandonment by the Dutch state. Their political subjectivities and precarious, liminal legal statuses are shaped by state regulations, labelling and coding, mobility restrictions and bordering practices predicated on exclusionary Westphalian categorisations of citizenship (e.g., Tazzioli 2020; Agamben 1998; Hyndman 2004, 2012; Hyndman and Giles 2011). Simultaneously, most are also forced to move through a series of camps while waiting for decisions on their applications in a 'protracted state of purgatory' (UNHCR 2006) and continuous disruption or dislocation (Rekenhamer 2018).

Perceptions of individuals living in asylum camps are often framed through exclusionary rhetoric that homogenises and categorises asylum seekers as passive and helpless, geopolitical and welfare threats, a non-citizen 'Other,' or framed asylum seekers as objectified victims (e.g., Cresswell 2006; Dempsey and McDowell 2019; Myadar 2021; Vayrynen 2017). Media reports and research on asylum seekers or refugees residing in European camps often present simplistic representations of places of sovereignty, power and victimisation, and examples of migrant agency remain understudied (e.g., Brun and Fabos 2015; Eastmond 2007; Ehrkamp 2017).

Contrary to this narrow view of migrant experiences, this article demonstrates how migrants routinely counter the state of surveillance, control and exclusion. This project draws from archival and original fieldwork conducted with asylum seekers in Dutch asylum camps, as well as those outside the asylum system who are designated as 'undeportables.' As many interviewees suggest, migrants actively challenge their situation and geopolitical subjectivities via resistance and agency, often through the production of grassroot networks that transcend the physical borders of the camps.

Indeed, asylum seekers display numerous and innovative methods of advocacy networks and agency within, across and beyond the borders of asylum camps in an attempt to challenge their experiences. In this regard, the asylum camps can also be regarded as sites of generative struggles where alternative agencies are produced; and, despite various forms of control and subjectivity. The following work focuses on asylum seekers in the Netherlands since 2015 when the state witnessed a notable increase in the number of migrants (Figure 1: GIS maps of asylum applications over time). This article also highlights how camps can become the intersection of key forms of geopolitical control of asylum seekers (e.g., surveillance, segregation and exclusion), with that of migrant agency and networks forged within and beyond asylum camps to challenge these conditions.

This is also true for those who are politically remade by a state's rejection of their asylum claims, such as an 'undeportables'. These individuals, commonly called 'illegals' in the Netherlands, are often stateless individuals or persons who do not possess official documents (e.g., passports or other adequate documentation) to establish their nationality or country of origin. Without the necessary documentation, the Dutch state cannot identify where each individual needs to be 'returned' and, therefore, cannot deport these individuals. These bureaucratic expectations reveal a Westphalian perception of

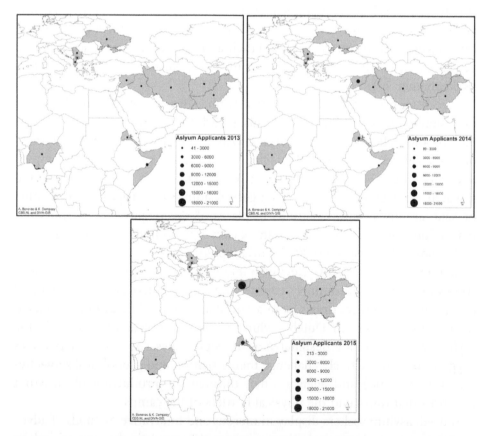

Figure 1. Largest applicant states' rapid increase in asylum applications to the Netherlands (2013–2015).

citizenship, which fails to recognise that some individuals do not possess birth certificates or passports.[2] Indeed, Netherlands' 'undeportable' migrants are individuals who are no longer permitted within asylum camps, mandated to leave the host state, but cannot legally be deported. Instead of disappearing into the shadows, many 'underportables' in the Netherlands have united to launch an international social media campaign to gain recognition for their struggle for asylum, challenging the categorisation of 'rejected asylum seeker,' and extending the advocacy networks that were established in the asylum camps beyond their physical boundaries.

This article thus examines often overlooked production of migrant agency networks in response to their lived experience of embodied geopolitical violence of control, categorisation and exclusion that is produced in the various spatialities of asylum seeking. To do so, the article relies on feminist geopolitics as a framework to understand how migrants counter their geopolitical subjectivities via agency (and corresponding networks) fostered within and extending beyond camp borders. Feminist geopolitics is useful in this investigation because it draws attention to the experiences of the disenfranchised across multiple geopolitical scales, including the body as the most intimate site (e.g., Hyndman 2019; Hiemstra 2019; Koopman 2011; Mountz and Hyndman 2006; Myadar and Davidson 2020a. In this way, it brings the geopolitics of human and affective matter to the forefront while highlighting migrant diversity, agency and strategic contestation of the asymmetry of power and policing (e.g.; Dowler and Sharp 2001; Hyndman 2004; 2019; Lee and Pratt 2012).

This article advances the understanding of feminist geographical engagement with respect to its empirical, epistemological and ontological intersections of migration, camps and power to interrogate forms of geopolitical control, marginalisation and the everyday life(s) of 'dislocated temporality,' (e.g., McNevin 2019; Shindo 2019) as well as migrant agency, both within and beyond camp borders. Feminist geopolitics argues that a state-centred approach of spaces of violence in camps fails to attend to embodied and emotional landscapes of asylum seekers (e.g., Katz 2001).

Examples of migrant agency are often embedded in diverse advocacy networks, social media campaigns, self-promotion and grassroots non-violent securities (e.g., Lee and Pratt 2012; Koopman 2011). This is an important avenue for problematising the effects of segregation and ostracisation of asylum seekers who are trapped in interim zones of confinement. Indeed, by examining embodied migrant experiences and advocacy networks that exist both in and outside of camps, this paper frames Dutch asylum camps not only as sites of control and violence but also as places in which migrants produce alternative agencies and advocacy networks that transcend camp borders and challenge subjectivity through Dutch asylum procedures.

The following discussion is organised in four main sections. The first section highlights theoretical discussions of state control of asylum seekers, as well as migrant agency and counter-hegemonic efforts in and beyond camp boundaries. The second describes the methodology utilised for data collection and analysis. The third section, which draws on interview data, investigates examples of Dutch geopolitical control of migrants and migrant efforts to resist and counteract subjectivity by the state. The fourth section reflects on the data presented in the article and offers suggestions for subsequent research.

Geopolitical Control and Migrant Agency in and beyond the Borders of Asylum Camps

EU member-states employ an array of spatial strategies to control migrants and international irregular migration including militarisation and privatisation of migration control, offshore processing and detention centres and increased surveillance in asylum camps where migrants often wait in inhospitable and impermanent living conditions (e.g., Gill, Conlon, and Oeppen 2014; Jones and Johnson 2016; Mountz 2011). As a result, migrants experience a variety of forms of geopolitical control as well as pervasive and varied forms of violence throughout migration and asylum processes (e.g., Dempsey 2020; McConnell et al., 2017; Jones 2016). I contend that by focusing on the lived experience of migrants under Dutch geopolitical control, and how camps can become sites of struggle where migrant advocacy is produced, we can better understand how individuals are influenced by and respond to migration policies (e.g., Dowler and Sharp 2001; Hiemstra 2012, 2019; Mountz 2004; Hyndman 2004; Silvey 2005). For example, asylum seekers' restricted mobility within a host state is highly political (e.g., Ashutosh 2012; McNevin 2019; Tazzioli 2020; Tsianos and Karakayali 2010). Their transitory legal status under immigration law regulates their movement and 'spatial positioning,' underpinned by states' political constructions of space 'Otherness' (Gupta and Ferguson 1992). Indeed, the spatial violence of these restrictions imposed on migrant bodies 'arrest' their movement within national borders and in camps where geopolitical hierarchical orderings are grounded in everyday life.

As migrant experiences within and 'in connection to' camps, which are distinct political and spatio-temporal spaces, academic investigations must 'engage the conditions of encampment or capture and the multiple practices through which refugees and asylum seekers escape or contest these techniques of policing and provisioning' (Opondo and Rinelli 2015, 932). In this way, scholarly investigations are more effectively able to highlight avenues of migrant agency, advocacy and resistance within and beyond camp borders. The avenues for migrant agency occur at the scale of an individual body (e.g., hunger strikes and lip sewing), within camps via advocacy groups and trans-camp and post-camp advocacy networks and social media campaigns that can occur in the camps as well as extend beyond physical camp borders (e.g., Bargu 2017).

There is a growing body of recent work that illuminates experiences of asylum seekers and refugees in the 'spatialities of the camp' (e.g., Davies and Isakjee 2015; Gilroy 2013; Katz 2016; Katz 2017; Minca 2015; Martin 2015; Maestri 2017; Ramadan 2013) and, more specifically, camps in Europe (e.g., Cuttitta 2012; Darling 2011; Rygiel 2011). Instead of homogeneous conceptualisations of camp space (conditions and structures vary greatly), scholarly attention focuses on particular geopolitical contexts, migrant diversity and mobilities, and migrant provisional legality (e.g., Casas-Cortes, et al. 2015; Feldman 2015; Hyndman 2012; Wilson 2014). The embodied geopolitical experiences that migrants encounter in camps are often contingent on 'nationality, social class, 'racial profile,' gender, their overall embeddedness within territorial political institutions and their place of residence' (Minca 2015, 80). However, examinations of camps as sites of migrant agency and advocacy networks remain understudied. This article aims to fill this gap.

Feminist geopolitics is well positioned to highlight migrant agency by looking beyond focusing solely on statecraft, thereby fostering the examination of individuals and agencies (e.g., Hakli and Kallio 2014; Koopman 2011). While anti-geopolitics, a branch within critical geopolitics, rejects elite practice(s) and focuses on 'geopolitics from below,' the resistance to political policies and institutions, representations and the media (Routledge 2003), feminist geopolitics re-envisions this resistance to emphasise who, how, what and at which scales (Dowler and Sharp 2001; Shindo 2019; Vayrynen, Pehkonen, and Vaittinen 2017). By highlighting the embodied experiences and practices of the disenfranchised, these individuals and their voices are made more discernible. Bodies, such as those of migrants, become the 'sites of performance in their own right' (Dowler and Sharp 2001, 169) as they work to overcome processes of control and marginalisation. For example, Hyndman (2007) encouraged feminist geopolitics to employ 'finer and coarser' examinations to reveal spaces of violence, safety of individuals and groups and mobility as a lens for spatial manifestations of geopolitical power. Thus, as individuals and groups who come together to advocate for change, work to challenge the spatial, material and embodied violence of state domination.

Methodology

This project draws from archival and original fieldwork conducted with asylum seekers between May and August of 2016 and 2017 in 15 Dutch asylum camps (39 1–3-h, semi-structured ethnographic interviews) and with seven 'undeportables' forced outside the asylum system. The research also included participant observations and interviews with camp ambassadors, local social workers, and Red Cross employees but focuses primarily on the ethnographic interviews with asylum seekers and 'undeportables' in the Netherlands. I conducted fieldwork in accordance with the Human

Subjects Protocol set by the Institutional Review Board for this project. Interview participants were recruited through networks via: camp ambassadors, the Red Cross, local social workers and the author in the field. Interviews occurred in private rooms in camps or at the local Red Cross facilities, based on interviewees' preferences. All interviews were conducted in the interviewee's language of choice and facilitated with a translator when necessary. I interviewed a diverse group of individuals from different countries of origin, age, class, family status, genders and religious/spiritual backgrounds. Each interview focused on lived experiences on campus and any efforts made by interviewees to counteract state control/legislation while seeking asylum in the Netherlands. All were catalogued anonymously[3] and transcribed for analysis. In order to unsettle the hierarchical power imbalances and relational positionalities of interviewing, these interviews were conducted utilising reciprocal interviewing (e.g., Dempsey 2018) through which participants were encouraged to ask about the interviewer's personal life.

Examples of Geopolitical Control and Exclusion of Asylum Seekers in the Netherlands

This section demonstrates how asylum camps become spaces of governmentality, surveillance, control, exclusion and embodied geopolitical violence for asylum seekers. This section also lays the groundwork for the following discussion of how migrants respond via counter-hegemonic efforts and/or resistance to their legal subjection by the state.

According to interviewees, asylum seekers experience geopolitical control in and beyond camps – institutionalised sites of corporal control – in multitude of ways, including technological forms of control, surveillance, categorisation, exclusion and segregation from city centres and local residents. For example, asylum seekers in the Netherlands are subjected to fingerprinting and a registration cycle in order to begin the asylum process (Rekenkamer 2018). A coalition of Dutch Border Police (KMar) and Alien Police (AVIM) are responsible for the initial process of identifying and registering migrants. Should international background checks reveal that a migrant possesses citizenship from a state that is geopolitically categorised as 'safe' (regardless of their individual situation within it), prior registration in another EU member-state (i.e., Dublin III Regulation 2013), or 'other questionable criteria' (www.gov.nl.immigration), the application is rejected and the individual is physically removed from the camp. Immigration regulations state that migrants from 'safe' countries will be rejected based upon pre-existing geopolitical relations. In these circumstances, it is extremely rare in the Netherlands for an asylum seeker's appeal to successfully overturn the initial rejection of their application (Rekenkamer 2018).

The variety of categorisations of temporary legal status for migrants in Europe has also proliferated greatly (e.g., Levy 2010). There are also categorial biases against certain individuals based on intrastate geopolitics. For example, while Syrian asylum seekers were identified as 'non-economic' migrants as a blanket category, those from Afghanistan or Eritrea were commonly labelled as 'economic' migrants[4] thus experienced higher rates of rejection of asylum (UNHCR 2019). As one interviewee from Afghanistan explained:

> My chances of gaining asylum would be much better for me if I was from Syria. The Dutch system treats Syrians better; they get separate application procedures and are granted asylum more often and faster than Afghans or Iraqis. I know some Afghans lose their ID papers and try say they are from Syria. Better treatment, better chances of asylum if they believe you (interview #22, 2016).

In the Netherlands, when individuals' applications are rejected, they are contacted by the Dutch Repatriation and Departure International Service (DT&V) and are subsequently deported. For those who were not initially rejected by KMar or AVIM, the Dutch Immigration and Naturalisation Service (IND) interviews the remaining asylum seekers to determine if their asylum claim is 'valid.' During this time, the applicants commonly face a protracted period of waiting for a decision on their application in camps where they are under a multitude of layered surveillance.

Dutch asylum camps are collectively administered by the Dutch Central Agency for the Reception of Asylum Seekers (COA). The COA governs all asylum camps, including providing sustenance, accommodation and medical care for the inhabitants – the quality of which has been questioned by many asylum seekers. The numerous forms of surveillance and control that asylum seekers are subjected to range from security cameras, digital tracking and weekly fingerprint checks in the camp's main office. This technologically driven biometric system provides greater legal and spatial control as it expunges migrants' individualities and reduces them to a single immigration ID number. Some of the camps' gates are opened with a resident migrant's fingerprint scan (personal interview #8, 2016), turning migrant bodies into state-registered biometric keys (e.g., Koshravi 2010). Additionally, if an individual does not complete a weekly fingerprint scan, they become ineligible to receive 1 week of benefits, including food stipends. These and other surveillance and monitoring tactics are just a few examples of methods that are used to control migrants.

The vast consequences of these and other dehumanising governance procedures that have materialised through technology can lead to an efficient removal or suspension of migrants' basic human rights and protections (e.g., Gill, Conlon, and Oeppen 2014). If the camp system requires an individual to relocate to a different camp throughout the Netherlands, migrants have no recourse against the transfer. As a result, some asylum seekers lived in 2–4 different Dutch camps during their waiting processes. According to all interviewees, such forced dispersals are confusing and frightening. As the spokesperson for the Asylum Seekers Alliance of Keipelgevangenis Camp argued:

> We believe these requirements and common policies are inhumane. We are scanned and IDed as if we are criminals or even farm animals. We have broken no laws by filing for asylum here, yet the government treats us like prisoners and denies us any form of human dignity while we wait for a decision on asylum' (personal interview #8, 2016.)

Migrants' mobility is a technique of state governance and control, which can be employed via detention, containment and/or dispersal throughout a host country. According to Tazzioli, this not only includes the frequent transfer of migrants through a series of camps but also by locating camps far from urban centres. Indeed, asylum seekers in the Netherlands are often geographically segregated from the general public due to the isolated locations of many asylum camps. Located in rural communities or on the outskirts of city centres, asylum seekers are forced to reside apart from the larger community and, often, at great distances from grocery markets or supply stores (e.g., Dempsey 2018). Thus, in this way, these camps set migrants apart in sites of exclusion, difference, temporality and stasis as they wait in legal limbo.

Indeed, many are forced to reside in temporary or makeshift constructions that range from tents, shipping containers and obsolete former prisons (COA 2017). The conditions reflect a sudden increase in asylum seekers in the Netherlands as well as the state's intentional efforts to appear less attractive as an asylum destination than Germany or Sweden (Tesfamariam 2017). Diverse populations of migrants (e.g., nationality, linguistic, cultural, religious, gender/sexual orientation, or age) are forced into these sites of capture – small and crowded rooms that afford no space for privacy, religious practices, or food preparation. This includes religiously adherent migrants' ability to gather communally to pray as COA regulations prohibit 'religious gatherings' in the camps (Tesfamariam 2017). As one interviewee pointed out, 'there are no common rooms where we are allowed to gather to pray in a group or in private' (interview #11, 2016). According to Tazzioli, these are tactics employed to prevent migrants from feeling 'settled' in place (2020, 11). As one male Afghan interviewee explained, he was assigned to a container camp in north-central Netherlands. He sleeps in a small and crowded room with three bunk beds full of men from different countries, religious and linguistic backgrounds:

> The room is always noisy and crowded. There is no space to sit or move around and we are always in each other's way. We do not all speak the same language, so it is hard to communicate, it is hard to sleep and hard to pray. Also, some hate the others in the room because of country of origin. The room is not a good place (interview #19, 2016).

As asylum seekers experience protracted waiting times for a decision on their applications (averaging between 9 months to 2 years, but many wait up to 4 years), their limited legal status within a host state restricts their mobility, privacy and many of their basic rights in what some have identified as a 'violent abandonment' by the state (e.g., Davies and Isakjee, 2003; Opondo and Rinelli 2015, 932). Indeed, all interviewees expressed regret, and in some cases resentment, for the time lost and potential opportunities as they waited for a decision on asylum. As one interviewee from Syria explained:

> Before the war, I was an engineer. I was productive. But now I wait and do nothing all day– they will not let me work and I cannot travel to Germany - nothing until they decide on my application. I called the Asylum Office to ask how much longer. They told me to wait more,
>
> there are many applications. I fear they will forget me (personal interview #31, 2016.)

The stress of the living conditions, traumatic experiences during/after their journey to Europe and the bureaucratic uncertainty of their asylum status contributes to many migrants' poor health (e.g., Dempsey 2020; Maillet, Mountz, and Williams 2016). There has been a high rate of suicides in the asylum camps, including 13 deaths and 80 attempts in the first half of 2014 alone (COA 2015). The imposed constraints are grounded in protracted liminalities and disruption, including the fact that most migrants are moved through many different camps before receiving a decision on their applications, which further increases migrant vulnerability within the state.

The geopolitical forces that produce and assign categorical labels to each migrant (e.g., refugee, asylum seeker, illegal immigrant, (un)deportable) present another form of violence inscribed on migrant bodies. Asylum seekers and refugees are constructed (i.e., made) and arrested through categorical labels that mark them as different. They are classified and discriminated as a migrant 'Other,' in essence constructing migrant bodies as discursive locations that are 'out of place' and transient within state sovereign borders (e.g., Gabrielatos and Baker 2008). These legal categorisations are also significant as they are utilised to distinguish host states' power and responsibility for each migrant (Maillet, Mountz, and Williams 2016). In addition, certain categorical labels deny or grant 'access to physical and social spaces (e.g., travelling within a country or between countries and being allowed to work) and resources' (Witteborn 2011, 1146). For example, Dutch laws do not permit asylum seekers to work or pursue specialised/higher education during this time, thereby producing individuals that are financially dependent on the host state.

In 2015, the Dutch government created a five-tiered multi-track policy to enable authorities to 'work more efficiently to turn down asylum applications from aliens abusing the asylum procedure' (Ministry of Security and Justice

2016, 2) and Dutch immigration laws also divide migrants between the following major geopolitical categories:

> An 'alien' is an individual that lacks Dutch citizenship (recognizing that not all have arrived to seek asylum); an 'asylum seeker' is an alien who applies for asylum; a 'deportable' is an alien with a rejected asylum application is order to leave (the term 'illegal' is applied if they refuse to leave); 'undeportable' is an alien whose asylum application is rejected, but cannot legally be deported; while 'refugee' is reserved for individuals who gain official status are permitted to remain within the Netherlands (Rekenhamer 2018, 12).

These categorical labels also cultivate an environment of exclusionary rhetoric and stereotypes, often based on primordial perceptions of differences within the public and the media. The European media has been instrumental in discursively invoking, producing and perpetuating geopolitical articulations of differences that liken migrant presence within European borders to an invasion (e.g., Dempsey and McDowell 2018). Under-age migrants are required to attend public schools, but they are labelled as 'aliens' [allochtonen] that often reaffirms and reinforces divisions between them and the rest of the student body. Many migrant interviewees reported experiencing forms of racial discrimination and targeted hate speech, such as 'terrorists', 'welfare thieves,' 'filth' by some of the members of the public, police and other government officials in the Netherlands (e.g., interviews #9, 2016 and #33, 2017).

These and similar exchanges have caused many migrants to feel threatened and trapped as they await a decision on their asylum papers. Indeed, as Witteborn argues, 'For some migrants, however, mobility is restricted by international and national laws as well as socio-political discourses, which regulate the migrant body and her ability to create social relations asylum seekers are spatially constructed and arrested through bureaucratic labelling and assignment to heterotopias and as a discursive location of transience and difference' (2011, 1142). In this way, migrant bodies are rendered as transient places of exceptionalism and exclusion within a host country.

In the politics of space and 'Otherness,' migrants are commonly 'stripped of their identities as individuals and re-subjectified as groups' (Mountz 2011, 386) along national and racial lines. The biases that underpin European categorisation of migrants also reflect significant racial and national discrimination. Particularly since 2015, Syrian migrants have been prioritised, 'fast tracked,' and in some cases provided separate accommodations and processing centres than the rest of irregular migrants entering Europe. Indeed, despite a variety of distinct conclusions, examinations of such geographies of exclusion reveal that many of these rulings are underpinned by racial and/or geopolitical prejudices (e.g., rejection of many Afghani, Iranian and Somali applications while 'fast-tracking' Syrians[5]). This hierarchical preference and priority treatment produce great resentment and tensions among some asylum seekers (e.g., personal interview #2, 6, 8, 11, 2016) and have also been condemned by the UN in recent reports (UNHCR 2016). In essence, migrants continue to be bound by the borders of their state of origin, for some producing a 'stigma' that can significantly influence their treatment within a host state as well as their chances of gaining asylum.

The state also functions as a 'gatekeeper' that determines which migrants are 'worthy' of asylum and which should be forcibly removed from its sovereign borders through decisions underpinned by racial and sexual discrimination. For example, the Dutch state and courts have ruled against asylum applications from individuals from Iraq unless the applicant is a homosexual, which is a crime in Iraq. Applicants who list sexual orientation as the impetus for their forced migration are subject to a particularly invasive line of questioning that can include questions such as: 'How long have you known that you were gay? Describe in detail how you knew that you were gay and how you have acted as a result. Have you ever had doubts about being gay? What have you done to accept yourself as gay? How has your sexual orientation affected your family?' However, in 2017, the Dutch IND rejected an application on the basis that the applicant 'was not gay enough' to merit asylum despite protests from the LGBT Asylum Support Organization in Amsterdam (Rainey 2017).

Migrant Agency and Counter-hegemonic Efforts in and beyond Camp Borders

While many assumptions pertaining to asylum seekers are often framed by passivity and helplessness (e.g., Malkki 1996), feminist geopolitics works to highlight embodied agency and counter-hegemonic efforts. By highlighting some of the 'lesser-known political struggles' (McNevin 2019) and specific forms of migrant solidarity, feminist geopolitics sheds light on the many ways in which migrants resist state control, exclusion and the conditions of their lived experiences. During extended periods of legal limbo under the state, many migrants actively challenge and negotiate the everyday geopolitical life that they encounter both in and outside of asylum camps. For example, Brun and Fabos (2015) demonstrate ways in which migrants actively 'make homes' during protracted displacement. The multi-scalar variety of counter-hegemonic efforts also includes protests at the level of the individual body (e.g., see Gill, Conlon, and Oeppen 2014 regarding hunger strikes and lip sewing), organising advocacy groups within a particular camp, or demanding system-wide structural changes within Dutch migration legislation. Feminist geographers have also drawn attention to migrant material practices, such as destroying passports or expunging their fingerprints, as a form of counter-hegemonic agency as well (e.g., Mountz 2011; Gill, Conlon, and Oeppen 2014; Malkki 1995).

According to interviewees, asylum seekers are becoming increasingly proactive in their resistance to state control and many of the bureaucratic processes they believe are unjust. Often facilitated through social media, several prominent migrant advocacy networks are forging new political spaces and offering new organising strategies for advocating for change. Some of their actions have resulted in modifications of Dutch immigration policies. One of the earliest successful campaigns focused on access to education. Previously, adult migrants were banned from participating in any form of employment or educational study in the Netherlands until/unless their asylum applications were approved. Recognising the importance of possessing the ability to understand and speak Dutch during the asylum application process, migrants of various nationalities and creeds organised protests to demand access to Dutch language classes in asylum camps before receiving a decision on their asylum application (e.g., personal interview #5, 8, 12, & 34, 2016, 2017). After significant campaigning (in person and social media platforms, such as Facebook and Twitter), and supplemental pressure from local NGOs and supportive government agencies (e.g., Wetenschappelijke Raad voor het Tegeringsbeleid), adult asylum seekers gained the right to study Dutch in camps (e.g., personal interview #8, 2016).

The significance of this accomplishment should not be overlooked. As one of the social workers that supported this campaign stated, 'gaining local language knowledge empowers and strengthens migrants' ability to self-advocate, make more-informed decisions, and establish and facilitate support networks across a variety of migrant nationalities' (personal interview #22, 2016). While this is a challenging undertaking, particularly due to the variety of linguistic and educational diversity present among asylum seekers (Van Heelsum 2017), many of their self-organised advocacy groups also work to ameliorate these gaps through in-camp tutoring and provide donated and/or publicly available technology (e.g., low-cost smartphones or access to public/library computers) to those who do not possess their own (e.g., personal interview #2, 2016).

Other organising strategies include those who actively work together to document and share their experiences through print, social media and/or scholarly publications to garner attention, raise awareness and advocate for legislative change. For example, because the Dutch Koepelgevangenis asylum camp is housed in a former prison, many of its inhabitants organised an advocacy group to argue that their bleak accommodations were both inhumane and reinforced xenophobic beliefs that 'migrants are criminals' and that seeking asylum was a criminal activity. This organisation also began working with local social workers and lawyers to campaign for better treatment, transportation to the city centre, improved housing accommodations (physical structures and personal privacy), racial/ethnic equality among asylum applications and access to education while awaiting asylum decisions. They contacted the municipal mayor and invited him to tour the camp facilities to witness their living conditions. Among the many suggestions, they asked the mayor to consider the removal of weekly fingerprint scans, suggesting that it frames asylum seekers as prisoners, unnecessarily subjugating migrants and reinforcing the perception that asylum seeking is a crime.

Over time, their actions raised awareness among the local community and subsequently gained some support for their campaign. As the leader of this advocacy group explained:

> We have seen an increase of local community members volunteering here. They come and offer free language classes and 'language tables' to help migrants learn and practice Dutch. Others come to assist with legal paperwork, advocate for sponsorship by a local business (who might pay for private accommodations), and offer transportation and advise to their required immigration meetings during the asylum process. Recently, a 'watch dog agency' started tracking and documenting ethnicity in accepted asylum applications in order to publicize ethnic bias in the Dutch asylum system (personal interview #3, 2016).

In addition, the local government agreed to add a new bus stop at the entrance of the camp in order to increase migrant mobility and access to the city centre. Engineers were tasked with evaluating possibilities for structural and personal-privacy improvements within camps.

This and similar advocacy groups forge and maintain networks that originated within camps and now extend beyond camp boundaries, highlighting the importance of social advocacy and collective agency. For example, members contact former asylum seekers that gained asylum within the Netherlands to encourage them to return to the camps as volunteers, help others navigate the asylum process and/or serve as 'witnesses' in the camp to hold administrators accountable for camp living conditions. Others have become public speakers or met with lawmakers to advocate for legislative changes for asylum seekers and other irregular migrants in the Netherlands. As Lee and Pratt's 2012 work demonstrated, similar examples of solidarity highlight the importance of social relations and networks in regard to how migrant agency is conceptualised, produced and employed.

Increasingly, asylum seekers have opted to widely publicise their protests. For example, some publicly protested their living conditions in the streets of major Dutch cities, such as Amsterdam, in hopes of gaining sympathy and support from their campaign. Many advocacy groups believe that utilising official bureaucratic channels and social/print media via technology is a more successful approach for reaching a larger audience (interview with the head of the Dutch Asylum Seekers Alliance, May 2017). Social media continues to offer migrants new avenues of communication in which they can receive and exchange information. They can also express their opinions and personal experiences to a global audience. Many utilise technology in their various avenues of resistance to facilitate navigating bureaucratic red tape, communicate with other asylum-seekers, teach new arrivals in camps, as well as publicise their stories and share information about their living conditions within the camps in order to demand improvements and legislative changes. Increasingly, the implemented improvements within a particular camp (e.g., Keipelgevangenis Camp) are shared as a precedent from which other camps may utilise to advocate for similar improvements as well.

This technological knowledge also facilitates the creation of new migrant advocacy groups. For example, as migrants increasingly share knowledge about camp conditions, accommodations and experiences in person and via social media and individuals utilise this data to lobby within their own camp for improved facilities, treatment or accommodations. Others employ mobile apps to identify safe places to shop and recreate [what] near their camps (e.g., visit-related asylum forums). As one interviewee explained, 'I read Facebook reports by other migrant groups to learn which market stores are safe for me to shop. If there were any problems on the bus or in the city centre when they were there. After I read, I go where I will not be bothered or harassed' (personal interview #5, 2016).

While not all asylum seekers cooperate or even interact with one another in the camps, it is notable that a number of individuals from diverse nationalities, ethnicities, religions, genders and ages actively choose to collaborate over these platforms despite these disparities. Particularly through the use of technology, asylum camp advocacy groups and refugees have reached larger audiences, maintained contact and continue to collaborate on national migrant advocacy campaigns. McNevin (2019, 13) has also demonstrated how 'transformational solidarity' can connect groups of individuals that are 'too often pitted against each in ways that obscure shared forms of oppression and the potential for common political platforms.'

While the spatial violence imposed on asylum seekers regarding mobility and surveillance within camps produces a space of state governance and social exclusion from the general public primarily through isolation and ostracisation, the borders of these interim zones of confinement do not represent the geographical limit of diverse forms of embodied violence experienced by migrants within the Netherlands. Indeed, there are migrants who are excluded or expulsed from the physical boundaries of asylum camps. This is particularly true for migrants who are administratively barred from their premises if their asylum applications are rejected. In this way, asylum camps consequently become spaces of greater exclusion that subject 'rejected' asylum seekers to removal and often eventual deportation – 'a secondary instrument of migration control' (Gibney 2008, 147). However, the migrant networks and advocacy practices fostered within camps extend beyond their borders, particularly for 'undeportables' migrants. Indeed, there is a significant 'deportation gap' between those who are authorised for deportation and those who the state actually removes. This includes individuals who cannot obtain residency permits in the Netherlands (and cannot apply for asylum in a different EU member-state), but who cannot physically be returned to their country of origin – known as an 'undeportable'.

The state marginalises 'undeportables' by barring them access to migrant reception centres or asylum camps. They are also commonly apprehended by the police, imprisoned or forced to live on the streets without state support. Subsequently, they are subjected to a cycle of arrests, detentions and 'expulsion attempts' only to eventually be returned to the streets. Indeed, in recent years, the Dutch government has increased the number of detentions of irregular migrants, but not the number of deported migrants (Rekenkamer 2018). The impact of this embodied geopolitical violence for many migrants has manifested in an increase in physical and mental health illnesses (e.g., Dempsey 2020). According to Amnesty International:

> More than half of the country's 'undeportable' irregular migrants and rejected asylum-seekers cannot be legally expelled and are often left destitute after having gone through the Dutch asylum procedure and detention system. Although the numbers are inevitably rough estimates, human rights organizations report that there are currently approximately 35,000 to 60,000 people living in the Netherlands illegally who de facto cannot be deported even when apprehended by immigration authorities ... Having exhausted all judicial possibilities of remaining legal resident in the Netherlands, thousands of people, including families with children, are simply put on the street and told to leave the country within 48 hours (cited in Brechenmacher et al., 2012, 2).

Yet, in spite of the systemic state-sanctioned violence these individuals experience, many 'undeportables' have self-organised with others from their former asylum camp(s) of similar geopolitical fate in resistance to Dutch policies of exclusion. Many begin organising before they are forced out of the camps or utilising social media to communicate and strategize, and many of these individuals chose to publicly protest their violent rejection by the state. Their practice of refusal demonstrates powerful critiques of Dutch citizenship and naturalisation regulations, and their strategy to publicly challenge the state's current immigration legislation forges new spaces of politics that extend beyond granted citizenship or within the perimeter of an asylum camp.

Their first substantial protest, 'Refugees-on-the-Street,' began during the spring of 2011. These protestors established informal networks for support and information (e.g., Support Committee for Undocumented Workers OKIA), organised public campaign sit-ins in Amsterdam and the Hague, as well as street demonstrations with large banners with their slogan, 'WE ARE HERE'. Their intentional employment of the term 'refugee' also exemplifies their counter-hegemonic claims within the Dutch asylum system. By self-identifying as 'refugees,' they are actively refuting the legitimacy of the Dutch state's rejection of their asylum and humanitarian requests as they endeavour to gain support for their protest campaign.

By 2014, this group launched an international campaign under their slogan 'WE ARE HERE' (WIJ ZIJN HIER) and developed a Facebook and webpage to raise awareness of their transgressive struggles, shared situation(s), as well as the unique gendered experiences among the 'undeportables.' For example, while some churches, NGOs and migrant advocacy groups, such as Open Door (Wereldhuis), LOS (National Support for the Undocumented) or Vluchtelingenwerk are dedicated to helping these migrants, they cannot support all these individuals' needs. They also stress the added elements of vulnerability for female and transgender 'undeportables' as many of the aforementioned support facilities have limited or no capacity to assist women and transgendered individuals. Subsequently, drug and sex traffickers have increasingly targeted these 'undeportables' in the Netherlands (Brechenmacher et al., 2012). Ultimately, their goal is to raise awareness of their geopolitical and physical vulnerabilities as well as advocate for legislative change in the Dutch asylum system. As their website proclaims:

> We decided to make the inhumane situation that we have to live in – visible; by no longer hiding and illustrating what Dutch regulations and the 'asylum gap,' [not receiving aid, but cannot be deported] which is the root of our problems, are doing to refugees. Visit our website and Facebook for our press releases, reports and important announcement. You can also meet us in person.[6]

Through their social media and public campaigns, WE ARE HERE collectively work to challenge the accuracy and exclusionary enforcement practices of the Dutch asylum system, migrant categorical labels and the state's ability to bypass what they believe are their basic human rights afforded by the 1951 Geneva Convention. They are also creating new connections among other migrants and others who share in solidarity. As one 'undeportable' in Amsterdam explained: 'My human rights were violated by the Dutch military police and the State Secretary [Staatssecretaris] is aware of the violations and refused to do anything to help me. All I ask now is for basic shelter, but the Dutch government will not provide it to me. When I used social media, people heard and many have offered to help me' (personal interview #39, 2017).

Through cooperation and collaboration, technology and local support, WE ARE HERE is working to re-map the geographies of exclusion in the Netherlands. They actively campaign for a right to asylum, to work and to forge places of belonging within a state that has declared them 'placeless.' Indeed, the aforementioned protest campaigns and advocacy networks are only some of the examples of the various forms of migrant agency present within and beyond camp borders as migrants actively negotiate and respond to the embodied violence and abandonment they experience at the hands of the Dutch state.

Conclusion

While increased mobility is a core tenet of a progressively globalising world, nevertheless, governance of human mobility is also a discriminatory and highly regulated mechanism in international geopolitics and political economy. This is particularly true for forced migrants whose movement and categorisation are highly political and restricted within a host state. Media discourses and xenophobic rhetoric inscribe and construct migrant bodies as alien, transient, threatening and marked as a site of difference. Asylum seekers are relegated to asylum camps where they remain under surveillance, scrutinised and forced to endure liminal temporality and extended wait times for the Dutch state's decision on their application. The effects of this segregation and abandonment by the state are widespread and contribute to the production of camps as places of discursive and physical marginalisation and sites of spatial production of geopolitical control and exclusion.

Despite these conditions, many migrants actively challenge these experiences via resistance and agency, such as the production of grassroots advocacy networks that extend within and beyond the physical borders of the camps. This article advances conceptualisations of asylum camps beyond a simplistic perception of a site of power and control, but also a site of struggle where migrant advocacy networks are produced. In this way, camps can also be seen as distinct political spaces in which migrants' sovereign subjugation is negotiated and challenged, counter-hegemonic acts are performed and where diverse migrant collaborative advocacy networks are forged, grounded and stretch beyond camp borders. Additionally, instead of presenting migrants as passive victims of the asylum system, the article has relied on feminist geographic frameworks to bring examples of human agency and affective matter within the geopolitics of asylum to the forefront.

This paper has highlighted examples of how migrants negotiate, resist and navigate the challenges of living in geopolitically situated subjectivity, both physically and digitally. Through their individual and networked advocacy groups, they subvert hegemonic geopolitical discourses and categorisations of migrants within the global geopolitical contexts of xenophobia that underpins the construction of political differences and irreconcilability. This includes the 'undeportables' many of whom continue to publicly advocate for their most basic human rights and challenge hierarchical constructions of illegality. Their actions provide examples of political agency and claims of belonging that exist outside of narrow legislation and categorisations of citizenship. Their struggles also underscore the asymmetry of power embedded in Dutch migration policy and state practices that regularly refute the humanitarian values and principles to which the Netherlands subscribes. As this paper is based on case studies, further research is required. Future research could engage the intersection(s) of migrant agency and other states' measures of migration control, particularly in response to COVID-19 quarantines and budgetary restructuring.

Despite inequities and human rights violations, many migrants remain undaunted as they publicly campaign for basic rights and actively contribute to their local communities through volunteer projects, such as urban renewal programmes and elder care (Wij Zijn Hier 2016). Such examples further highlight many asylum seekers' bravery and strategic resistance to geopolitical subjectivity and control.

Notes

1. This interviewee was an asylum seeker in this camp and organised a grassroot alliance that advocates for better living conditions and access to education during the asylum process.
2. Other rulings include: rejected asylum seekers from failed states such as Syria, Ethiopia or Eritrea must be returned to their origin state voluntarily; states currently under a travel ban; citizens of former states such as Yugoslavia; or states that refuse to accept or assist in the return of its citizens (European Commission 2018).
3. The only exception was interview #8, who requested to be identified as the Spokesperson of the Camp Alliance.
4. These categorisations, appointed during the asylum application process, reflect the Dutch government's claim that Afghanistan or Eritrea are "safe" countries of origin.
5. For annual asylum reports and registration procedures see European Commission 28 March, 2018.
6. Translation by author, website accessed 5/6/2017.

References

Agamben, G. 1998. *Homo sacer: Sovereign power and bare life*. Stanford: Stanford University Press.
Bargu, B. 2017. The silent exception: Hunger striking and lip-sewing. *Law, Culture and the Humanities* May 1–28. doi:10.1177/1743872117709684
Brechenmacher, S., Kapoor, D. and van Lindert, T., 2012. The Undeportables: An insight into the invisible lives of "undeportable" migrants in the Netherlands.
Brun, C., and C. Fabos. 2015. Making homes in limbo? A conceptual framework. *Refuge* 31 (1):5–17. doi:10.25071/1920-7336.40138.
Casas-Cortes, M. 2015. Riding routes and itinerant borders: Autonomy of migration and border externalization. *Antipode* 47 (4):894–914. doi:10.1111/anti.12148.
Cresswell, T. 2006. *On the move*. New York: Routledge.
Cuttitta, P. 2012. Lo spettacolo del confine: Lampedusa. *Trasformazione* 1 (2):187e195.
Darling, J. 2011. Domopolitics, governmentality and the regulation of asylum accommodation. *Political Geography* 30 (5):263–71. doi:10.1016/j.polgeo.2011.04.011.
Davies, T., and A. Isakjee. 2015. Geography, migration and abandonment in the calais refugee camp. *Political Geography* 49:93–95. doi:10.1016/j.polgeo.2015.08.003.
Dempsey, K. E. 2018. Negotiated positionalities and ethical considerations of fieldwork on migration: Interviewing the interviewer. *ACME: An International Journal for Critical Geographies* 17 (1):88–108.

Dempsey, K. E. 2020. Spaces of violence: A Typology of the political geography of violence against migrants seeking asylum in the EU. *Political Geography* 72:102–57.

Dempsey, K. E., and S. McDowell. 2019. Disaster Depictions and geopolitical representations in Europe's migration 'Crisis'. *Geoforum* 98:153–60. doi:10.1016/j.geoforum.2018.11.008.

Dowler, L., and J. Sharp. 2001. A feminist geopolitics? *Space and Polity* 5 (3):165–76. doi:10.1080/13562570120104382.

Eastmond, M. 2007. Stories as lived experience: Narratives in forced migration research. *Journal of Refugee Studies* 20 (2):248–64. doi:10.1093/jrs/fem007.

Ehrkamp, P. 2017. Geographies of migration I: Refugees. *Progress in Human Geography* 41 (6):813–22. doi:10.1177/0309132516663061.

European Commission. 2018. *EU facility for refugees in Turkey: The commission proposes to mobilise additional funds for Syrian refugees*, March 18 http://europa.eu/rapid/press-release_IP-18-1723_en.htm

Feldman, I. 2015. What is a camp? Legitimate refugee lives in spaces of long-term displacement. *Geoforum* 66:244–52. doi:10.1016/j.geoforum.2014.11.014.

Gill, N., T. Conlon, and N. Oeppen. 2014. The tactics of asylum and irregular migrant support groups. *Annals of Association of American Geographers* 104 (2):373–81. doi:10.1080/00045608.2013.857544.

Gilroy, P. 2013. *Between camps: Nations, cultures and the allure of race*.

Hakli, J., and K. Kallio. 2014. Subject, action and polis: Theorizing political agency. *Progress in Human Geography* 38 (2):181–200. doi:10.1177/0309132512473869.

Hiemstra, N. 2012. Geopolitical reverberations of U.S. migrant detention and deportation: The view from Ecuador. *Geopolitics Special Issue: Migration, Mobility and Geopolitics* 17 (2):293–311.

Hiemstra, N. 2019. *Detain and deport: The chaotic U.S. immigration enforcement regime*. Athens: University of Georgia Press (Geographies of Justice and Social Transformation series).

Hyndman, J. 2004. Mind the gap: Bridging feminist and political geography through geopolitics. *Sociology*. doi:10.1016/j.polgeo.2003.12.014.

Hyndman, J. 2012. The geopolitics of migration and mobility. *Geopolitics* 17 (2):243–55. doi:10.1080/14650045.2011.569321.

Hyndman, J. 2019. Unsettling feminist geopolitics: Forging feminist political geographies of violence. *Gender, Place and Culture* 26 (1):3–29. doi:10.1080/0966369X.2018.1561427.

Hyndman, J., and W. Giles. 2011. Waiting for what? The feminization of asylum in protracted situations. *Gender, Place, & Culture* 18 (3):361–79. doi:10.1080/0966369X.2011.566347.

Jones, R., and C. Johnson. 2016. Border militarisation and the re-articulation of sovereignty. *Transactions of the Institute of British Geographers* 41 (2):187–200. doi:10.1111/tran.12115.

Katz, C. 2001. On the grounds of engagement: A topography for feminist political engagement. *Signs* 26 (4):1213–34. doi:10.1086/495653.

Katz, I. 2016. A network of camps on the way to Europe. Forced Migration Review 51: 17–18.

Katz, I. 2017. Between bare life and everyday life: Spatializing Europe's migrant camps. *Architecture_MPS* 12:2.

Koopman, S. 2011. Alter-geopolitics: Other securities are happening. *Geoforum* 42 (3):274–84. doi:10.1016/j.geoforum.2011.01.007.

Koshravi, S. 2010. *The 'Illegal' traveller: An auto-ethnography of borders*. Palgrave Macmillan.

Levy, C. 2010. Refugees, Europe, camps/state of exception: "into the zone," the EU and extraterritorial processing of migrants, refugees, and asylum-seekers. *Refugee Survey Quarterly* 29 (1):92–119. doi:10.1093/rsq/hdq013.

Maestri, G. 2017. The contentious sovereignties of the camp: Political contention among state and non-state actors in Italian Roma camps. *Political Geography* 60:213–22. doi:10.1016/j.polgeo.2017.08.002.

Maillet, P., A. Mountz, and K. Williams. 2016. Researching migration and enforcement in obscured places: Practical, ethical and methodological challenges to fieldwork. Social and Cultural Geography 18: 2–24.

Malkki, L.H. 1996. Speechless emissaries: Refugees, humanitarianism, and dehistoricization. *Cultural Anthropology 11*: 377–404.

Martin, D. 2015. From spaces of exception to 'campscapes': Palestinian refugee camps and informal settlements in Beirut. *Political Geography* 44 (1):9–18. doi:10.1016/j.polgeo.2014.08.001.

McNevin, A. August 2019. 2019 Mobility and its discontents: Seeing beyond international space and progressive time. *Environment and Planning C: Politics and Space*. August. doi:10.1177/2399654419871966

Minca, C. 2015. Geographies of the camp. *Political Geography* 49:74–83. doi:10.1016/j.polgeo.2014.12.005.

Ministry of Security and Justice. 2016. Letter of 26 May 2016 from the state secretary for security and justice to the house of representatives. *House of Representatives* 19 (637):2257. (2015-2016).

Mitchell, K. 2006. Geographies of identity: The new exceptionalism. *Progress in Human Geography* 30 (1):95–106. doi:10.1191/0309132506ph594pr.

Mountz, A. 2011. Where asylum-seekers wait: Feminist counter-topographies of sites between states. *Gender, Place & Culture* 18 (3):381–99. doi:10.1080/0966369X.2011.566370.

Mountz, A., and J. Hyndman. 2006. Feminist approaches to the global intimate. *Women's Studies Quarterly* 34 (1–2):446–63.

Myadar, O. 2020. Place, displacement and belonging: The story of Abdi. In *Geopolitics*, 1–16.

Myadar, O., and R. A. Davidson. 2020a. Remembering the 'comfort women': Geographies of displacement, violence and memory in the Asia-Pacific and beyond. In Gender, place & culture, 1–23

Myadar, O., and R. A. Davidson. 2020b. Mom, I want to come home": Geographies of compound displacement, violence and longing. *Geoforum* 109:78–85. doi:10.1016/j.geoforum.2020.01.009.

Opondo, S., and L. Rinelli. 2015. Between camps/between cities: movement, capture and insurrectional migrant lives. *Globalizations* 12 (6):928–42. doi:10.1080/14747731.2015.1100856.

Rainey, V. 2017. "Not gay enough': Dutch authorities challenge asylum-seekers to prove their sexuality. November 9. http://www.wlrn.org/post/not-gay-enough-dutch-authorities-challenge-asylum-seekers-prove-their-sexuality

Ramadan, A. 2014. Spatialising the refugee camp. *Transactions of the Institute of British Geographers* 38 (1):65–77. doi:10.1111/j.1475-5661.2012.00509.x.

Rekenkamer, A. 2018. Asylum inflow in the Netherlands in 2014-2016: A cohort of asylum seekers. *The Netherlands court of audit communications department*, The Hague.

Rygiel, K. 2011. Bordering solidarities: migrant activism and the politics of movement and camps at Calais. *Citizenship Studies* 15 (1):1–19. doi:10.1080/13621025.2011.534911.

Shindon, R. 2019. *Belonging in Translation: Solidarity and Migrant Activism in Japan*. Bristol: University Press.

Silvey, R. 2005. Borders, embodiment, and mobility: feminist migration studies in geography. In *A companion to feminist geography*, ed. L. Nelson and J. Seager:, 138–49. Blackwell Publishing.

Tazzioli, M. 2020. Governing migrant mobility through mobility: containment and dispersal at the internal frontiers of Europe. *Environment and Planning C: Politics and Space* 38 (1):3–19

Tesfamariam, A. 2017. A chat with Vincent of the Oisterwijk Asylum seekers center. *Diggit Magazine*. https://www.diggitmagazine.com/interviews/chat-vincent-oisterwijk-asylum-seekers-center

Tsianos, and Karakayali. 2010. Transnational migration and the emergence of the European border regime: An ethnographic analysis. *European Journal of Social Theory* 13 (3):373–87. doi:10.1177/1368431010371761.

UNHCR. 2019. *Refugee and migrants in Europe*. https://data2.unhcr.org/en/documents/download/72643

UNHRC. 2016. *Policy on alternatives to camps*. http://www.unhcr.org/protection/statelessness/5422b8f09/unhcr-policy-alternatives-camps.html

Vayrynen, P., K. Pehkonen, and Vaittinen. 2017. *Choreographies or resistance: Mobile bodies and relational politics*. Rowman and Littlefield.

WE ARE HERE (http://wijzijnhier.org/who-we-are/) accessed January 20, 2019

Wilson, A. 2014. Ambiguities of space and control: When refugee camp and nomadic encampment meet. Nomadic Peoples 18(1):38–60

Diaspora Geopolitics in Toronto: Tamil Nationalism and the Aftermath of War in Sri Lanka

Jennifer Hyndman, Amarnath Amarasingam, and Gayathri Naganathan

During the mid to late 1980s tens of thousands of Tamils from Sri Lanka sought and got asylum in Canada, forging the basis of the sizeable diaspora today. The Canadian state granted overwhelmingly positive decisions to Tamil refugee claimants based on evidence that the Government of Sri Lanka colluded in systematic violence against and killing of Tamil civilians who were not part of the militant separatist rebel group known as the Liberation Tigers of Tamil Eelam (LTTE). Canada continues to accept a majority of Tamil asylum seekers today, and hosts diaspora geopolitics – a less state-centric politics among diaspora members – 'from below'.

We introduce the term 'diaspora geopolitics', building on existing scholarship, to shift attention from securitisation discourse and states' preoccupation with extremism in immigrant diasporas to subjects and voices that narrate different meanings of nationalism and justice in the face of violence and displacement. By 'diaspora geopolitics,' we refer to everyday understandings and practices of protest and survival in relation to often distant constellations of power that produce war, violence, human rights abuses and the displacement. In deploying the term 'diaspora geopolitics' we aim to shift the conversation away from state-centric security discourse about extremism that securitises diaspora subjects towards everyday geopolitics of nationalism, violence, and displacement among subjects of civil society (Pain and Smith 2008).

People who live in exile as part of diasporas share particular geopolitical and personal histories of violence and displacement and have left their country of origin. Of course, a turn to 'diaspora geopolitics' does not entail a complete rejection of analyses of state practices, as members of diasporas narrate not only personal histories of violence and displacement, but also the statecraft inherent in such processes. Rather, an emphasis on 'diaspora geopolitics' allows for an examination of transnational politics that traverse conflict zones and the safer spaces of sanctuary where diasporas form in negotiating violence – that is, in the concrete, lived experiences of our interviewees. Nor are these diaspora geopolitics monolithic. As our data show, these shared experiences of geopolitical and personal histories of violence and displacement are experienced differently across generations and respondents. Likewise, individuals do not respond to them in the same way. The age at which one was displaced from their home country, for example, shapes an individual's narration of these personal and geopolitical processes (Fuglerud 1999).

This paper traces expressions of Tamil nationalism and belonging in Canada among people living in the highly variegated 'Tamil diaspora' of Greater Toronto after the end of war in Sri Lanka in May 2009. The Canadian residents canvassed in our study conveyed a shared sense of outrage towards the Government of Sri Lankan (GoSL) for the war crimes and human rights atrocities visited upon Tamils during the early months of 2009, but also during 26 years of militarised conflict between the GoSL and militant rebels prior to end of military conflict. The well-documented widespread violence and death fuels, we show, Tamil nationalism in the diaspora, yet this politics-at-a-distance creates a distinct, even liberal-democratic, version of nationalism. Expressions of nationalism in Canada are at times wary of the Liberation Tigers of Tamil Eelam, or LTTE, the separatist rebel group that fought against the Sri Lankan state, claiming itself the champion and sole protector of the Tamil people, but also critical of the Canadian state for failing to act during the massacre of Tamil civilians in 2009.

Tamils from Sri Lanka began seeking refuge in Canada in the 1980s when militant rebels from the largely Tamil north faced off against a predominantly Sinhalese nationalist state and military. In retaliation for a deadly ambush in the Northern Province that killed 13 soldiers by the 'Tamil Tigers', Tamil civilians faced pogroms and firebombing of their homes and businesses in Colombo, the capital, but the violence continued and spread (Harrison 2012; Whitaker 2016). Tens of thousands of people arrived in Canada as asylum seekers. Some joined family members in Canada; others immigrated through economic channels. Today, Canada hosts the largest Tamil diaspora from Sri Lanka outside that country (Amarasingam 2015). Based on publicly available government statistics, McNeely and Lough (2014) aggregate Canadian immigration data to create a top ten list of source countries for total immigration, not just asylum, over the period 2003 to 2012. Sri Lanka is on that list every year within the ten-year range. The International Crisis Group (2020) reports that political instability in Sri Lanka continues in 2020:

> The government is reluctant to address the legacy of civil war and authoritarian rule. Inter-ethnic relations remain fragile, with Sinhala majoritarianism resisting any accommodation of Tamil political claims and militant Buddhist groups' campaign of violence and hate speech against Muslims posing a considerable threat to the country's stability.

During the calendar year 2018, more than 71% of asylum seekers from Sri Lanka were granted positive decisions in Canada by the Immigration and Refugee Board that adjudicates refugee claims (Rehaag 2019).

Tamil Canadians hold political office at federal, provincial, and municipal levels, and work in a wide range of vocations. Many have ongoing ties to family in Sri Lanka, and were both horrified and mobilised by the widespread human rights atrocities and alleged war crimes visited upon Tamils in the Northern Vanni district of the country in 2009. An estimated 40,000 civilians were killed, and more than 300,000 interned in camps after the end of military conflict in May 2009 (Harrison 2012; Weiss 2012; Whitaker 2016). The research presented in this paper probes people's sense of Tamil nationalism, and their sense of belonging to Canada and to Sri Lanka in the Greater Toronto Area, in the wake of these civilian deaths and the end of military conflict in Sri Lanka. Government troops there defeated the Liberation Tigers of Tamil Eelam (LTTE) in May 2009, and then Tamils from the Vanni region were interned in Menik camp until September 2012 (BBC 2012; ICG 2010). The acute violence and humanitarian abuses during the 2009 phase of war in Sri Lanka were broadcast around the world. These events shaped the views of among members of the Tamil diaspora in Greater Toronto. Documented war crimes and human rights atrocities against Tamils in Sri Lanka affected people in Canada, and shaped their connections to Tamils in Sri Lanka and views of Tamil nationalism and the LTTE in this context. We consider how this violence and the war launched against civilians in Sri Lanka shaped 'diaspora geopolitics', a reference to the politics-at-a-distance among Tamils in Greater Toronto, many of whom fled violence themselves only to witness it play out again from the purview of their homes in Canada.

We place our study of the Tamil diaspora in the Greater Toronto Area in the context of diaspora geopolitics which traverse national borders and defy any monolithic conception of belonging to, or making a home in a single country. While we elaborate on diaspora geopolitics below, we do not suggest that there is one salient geopolitical discourse for a given diaspora. Historically situated geographies of political violence against minority ethnonational groups, militarised nationalisms, and related displacement vary within and across conflict zones that scatter people and the multiple destinations where they land (Thiranagama 2011; Mayer 2004; Van Hear 2005). Rather, we draw on research with and of the Tamil diaspora and our data to qualify our contributions. Our study seeks to understand transnational politics, identities, and belonging, including Tamil nationalism in Canada and opinions of the LTTE outside of Sri Lanka. Drawing on extensive interview and focus group transcripts with Tamils in Canada who escaped the war in Sri Lanka or were born in Canada of parents who left the country, we analyse their perceptions of the human rights atrocities and related expressions of Tamil nationalism in the context of militarised violence in Sri Lanka.

The events of September 11, 2001 in the U.S. ushered in the 'war on terror' discourse with new vehemence, as a legitimate precautionary threat to all states (Aradau and van Munster 2007). States that accept immigrants and refugees from countries where militarised conflict exists, like Canada, stand on guard for any criminal or extremist elements that may cross their borders and set up operations. This is *not*, however, what we mean by diaspora geopolitics. Terrorist concerns are national security issues that governments and their intelligence agencies manage. Since the 1990s the Canadian Government has monitored the activities of the LTTE (or Tamil Tigers) in Canada, probing fundraising efforts and money laundering allegations (Bell 2000, 2001; Hyndman 2003). In 2006, the then Conservative Government of Prime Minister Stephen Harper put the LTTE on its watch list of terrorist organisations. In 2010, Prapaharan Thambithurai, an LTTE fundraiser, was convicted of terrorist financing in Canada (Public Safety Canada 2018a). The LTTE is known to have extorted 'donations' from Tamil families and businesses in Canada to support the LTTE cause (Amarasingam 2015; CBC 2006). Extremism and violence *in* Canada, however, are very rare among diasporas from war-torn countries, like Sri Lanka (CID 2019).[1]

When the Government of Sri Lanka (GoSL) aimed to eradicate the LTTE in early 2009, it went on a mass offensive against Tamil civilians in the Northern Province at the same time. Diaspora geopolitics among Tamils in Canada were complicated and variegated, including protests decorated with LTTE flags but also liberal democratic approaches focused on human rights, UN sanctions, and non-violence. In no way do we define the liberal strategies employed by diaspora members as a victory for Canadian liberalism and human rights: the Canadian government of the day did little, if anything, to object to let alone stop the violence against Tamil civilians in Northern Sri Lanka. It was a government that had listed the Tamil Tigers as a terrorist organization in 2006 and was reluctant to demonstrate support for Tamils waving LTTE flags on Parliament Hill. Yet many segments of the Tamil diaspora in Canada, as our transcripts show, used democratic language, campaigns, and human rights frameworks to protest the 'killing fields' of Sri Lanka. In the absence of condemnation by the Canadian state, the Tamil diaspora and its Canadian allies stepped in to call attention to the widespread killing of up to 40,000 Tamil people (Harrison 2012). Whether intended or not, we contend that such tactics worked *to challenge, even reverse, the securitisation of Tamils in the diaspora* as threats themselves, casting them not as militant supporters of the LTTE and potential terrorists, but as Canadians concerned about war crimes, human rights atrocities, and a civilian massacre. Again, we do not promote this species of liberalism as a political panacea to securitisation, but view these tactics as a decisive approach by diaspora subjects to reframe their protest as against the wanton killing of Tamil civilians, not simply as separatist geopolitics that could be read as terrorist, risky or dangerous by states.

A Roadmap of Diaspora Geopolitics

We begin, first, by framing the notion of diaspora geopolitics, building on diverse bodies of scholarship about diaspora, distorted mobility, and the geopolitics that generate them. Once this theoretical stage is set, the political context for war in Sri Lanka is briefly traced, from the rise of a majority Sinhala nationalism after Sri Lankan independence to the emergence of the Liberation Tigers of Tamil Eelam (LTTE, or 'Tamil Tigers') as the dominant militant separatist group that would take on the Sri Lankan state, leading to the eventual departure of at least one million Tamils from Sri Lanka before the end of military conflict in 2009 (Collyer 2012). To contextualise the geopolitical context in which the Tamil diaspora emerges in Canada, we also juxtapose our study with one undertaken at roughly the same time, after the human rights atrocities against Tamil civilians occurred and the military conflict ended in Sri Lanka in 2009 (Monahan, Berns-McGown, and Morden 2014). We show how Monahan et al.'s research (2014) tends towards securitising racialized diasporas from conflict zones living in Canada by succumbing to the state-centric preoccupations with national security and extremism.

We then outline our methods and present selected findings based on extensive multi-year research with Tamil Canadians in the Greater Toronto Area (GTA). Drawing on interview transcripts with fifty-two people and four focus groups that include many more, Tamil nationalism in Canada and views of the Tamil Tigers in the country are analysed. While the war is officially over in Sri Lanka, violence against Tamils and Muslims in Sri Lanka continues (Thiranagama 2011; Amarasingam 2015; Rehaag 2019): unresolved disappearances fester, and lack of accountability for tens of thousands of civilian deaths during the first half of 2009 remains an open wound a decade after the end of military conflict (Whitaker 2016). In 2013, a community leader in Mullaitivu characterised life in the Wanni region of Northern Sri Lanka as a 'war without sound', referring to deep insecurity without the sounds of firearms or mortars (Hyndman 2013).

To Move or Not to Move: Re-Imagining Mobility and Diaspora as the Norm

Diasporas can be viewed as a barometer of geopolitics. Civilians who flee are the flotsam and jetsam of war and constitute diasporas that may be geographically disparate, located in multiple countries. In a radical re-imagination of the sedentarist assumptions of 'home' and the realist geopolitics of displacement, anthropologist Malkki (1992), sociologists Sheller and Urry (2006), and geographer Cresswell (2006) attempt to disrupt the idea that human movement is the *exception* to human settlement. In this vein, Cresswell (2006, 46) contends that, "[m]obility has become the ironic foundation for anti-essentialism, antifoundationalism and antirepresentation." Carter (2005) also critiques the hybridity and diaspora literature for failing to transcend the essentialised notions of place that it aims to transgress.

The idea that mobility is the new metaphysical norm in modern social and geographical life is an intellectually attractive and provocative, if a largely theoretical, one. What it conceals is the disparate intersectional power relations that shape the possibility of mobility (Jones 2016; Massey 1991). While assumptions of mobility as choice may be seen as the norm in stable, prosperous societies, Lubkemann (2008) warns that 'involuntary immobility' is more common in situations of displacement generated by violent conflict, especially for those who are poor. All persons are subject to the calculus of Massey's (1991) power-geometry, wherein gender, class, ability and other axes of power condition potential mobility. Containment and immobility may be more common for internally displaced persons than for those who can afford to depart for diaspora locations (Van Hear 2005; Castles, 2008). Thiranagama's (2011) reference to the 'shadow diaspora' – those who would like to flee Sri Lanka but cannot – is salient here.

Between mobility and immobility, the more nuanced geopolitical concept of diaspora has captured the imagination of social scientists over the last two decades (Amarasingam 2016; Hyndman 2010). Coined originally in Greek as *diaspeirein* ('to scatter about, disperse'), the concept of diaspora has developed as a frame for understanding movements under conditions not of one's own making (Abraham 2015; Fuglerud 1999). More precisely, the dispersion of Jews among Gentiles and the violent rupture and spread of African peoples across the Atlantic during the European slave trade are salient examples of people moving away from an established or ancestral homeland to flee violence (Merriam-Webster 2019; Shohat 2006).

'Refugee diasporas' (Van Hear 2005) refer to groups of people targeted with violence and forced to flee protracted conflicts and widespread human rights abuses. Many, though not all, Tamils from Sri Lanka left under conditions of insecurity or based on threats of death as a minority ethno-national group (Sriskandarajah 2005; Rehaag 2019). More recently, Van Hear et al. (2018) develop the idea of *refugia*, a kind of diaspora citizenship and belonging that grants one residency rights in a particular, often global North, country but citizenship is practiced within a diaspora governance structure. As we understand it, *refugia* blends transnational governance and a liberal democratic framework among diaspora subjects. It is an idea in progress, not yet a structure in place. The Transnational Government of Tamil Eelam (TGTE) was launched after the war ended in 2009, but has not been sustained (Amarasingam 2015, 142–168). The TGTE fashioned itself as a kind of floating government of elected representatives from every Tamil diaspora community in the world. However, due to factionalism and internal disagreements, as well as lack of support amongst youth activists, it has largely remained stagnant (Amarasingam 2015, 164). Van Hear's research history in Sri Lanka and with Tamil diaspora communities in London and Toronto influences this proposal of finding belonging in the diaspora and *non-violent* self-governance from a distance.

Likewise, Amarasingam (2016) emphasises the political subjectivity and mobilisation of diasporas. In other words, diasporic and transnational activist identities are not inevitable results of communities of people moving from one place to another. These identities are forged through crisis, organizational lobbying and mobilization, as well as the identity of young people who want to connect back to the struggles of "where they came from" (Amarasingam 2015, 171). Diasporic subjects are not merely *outcomes* of war, but politicised protagonists in their own right (see Crosby and Lykes 2019). As we show later in the paper, diaspora geopolitics are everyday understandings and practices of protest and survival by diaspora subjects, not states – an expression of geopolitics from below (see Sharp 2011, 2019).

The Context of Tamil Displacement

Since the anti-Tamil pogroms of 1983, an estimated one million Tamils have left Sri Lanka (Collyer 2012). While dozens of countries have become new homes for them (Fuglerud 1999; Sriskandarajah 2005), Canada – as noted – hosts the largest Tamil diaspora from Sri Lanka with upwards of 300,000 members (Amarasingam 2015).

From late 2008 to May 2009, the Sri Lankan armed forces faced off against the LTTE in Mullivaikkal, a small spit of land near the coast of northeastern Sri Lanka, with hundreds of thousands of Tamils civilians caught in the crossfire, also known as 'the cage' (Weiss 2012). Meanwhile, in the Greater Toronto Area (GTA) a large number of resident Tamils with connections to Sri Lanka took to the streets. Peaceful demonstrations and an impressive 'human chain' were organised, calling for international attention to the violence in Northern Sri Lanka and a forceful rebuke of these attacks on humanitarian targets, such as hospitals, schools used as shelters and civilian spaces. The human chain of solidarity with Tamils in Sri Lanka was formed across Toronto's downtown. In April 2009, some 30,000 people protested the violence on Parliament Hill in Ottawa, yet little attention was paid by the Canadian Government to the public events highlighting and protesting acute violence in Sri Lanka against Tamils. As above, some of the those protesting the attacks on civilians in hospitals and schools were flying the LTTE flag, an organisation the Government had listed as 'terrorist' three years earlier (CBC 2009a; Amarasingam 2015, 97–141).

A bolder if more contested approach was taken in early May 2009 when some thousands of protesters blocked the Gardiner Expressway, a major thoroughfare in the city (Nallainathan 2009; Ashutosh 2013). According to some of our research participants, this action was considered too aggressive and unlawful, and many chose not to participate. The presence of the LTTE flag at this protest was also controversial, as we discuss below, with some of our informants expressing concern that separatist flags politicised the urgent issue of human rights atrocities happening in Sri Lanka. The tension between a militant separatist Tamil nationalism and a liberal democratic Tamil nationalism focused on human rights atrocities and war crimes is palpable. The media splash publicising the Gardiner Expressway protest was instant, though public responses to the protest – which halted traffic on a major Toronto commuting thoroughfare for hours – were mixed, in part related to the LTTE flags and how they were interpreted by Torontonians who knew that the organisation had been placed on the terrorist watch list (CBC 2009b; Hunter 2016).

Just as transnational political groups like the LTTE and the World Tamil Movement (WTM) can be listed by states as terrorist organisations, diasporas themselves can become the object of state suspicion, merely by coming from a country at war. The politics of *potential* extremism is thus noteworthy in the Tamil context: the creation of threat – the risky diaspora – can generate its own geopolitical imagination that casts diaspora members as potential terrorists. A national telephone survey of several thousand people by Monahan, Berns-McGown, and Morden (2014) asked respondents whether people immigrating to Canada from war zones 'import conflict'. Fifty-seven per cent said they thought so. While we do not wish to give much space or time to this flawed and leading question, the same study interviewed 220 people – including Tamils, Muslims and Sinhalese immigrants from Sri Lanka – and from other diasporas. None showed evidence that extremism is 'imported' alongside immigration. The Monahan, Berns-McGown, and Morden (2014) study does provide a cautionary tale to researchers studying extremism, terrorism, and geopolitics of diasporas from a state perspective. The very act of asking research questions can cast racialized aspersions on diasporas and raise public concerns about the potential insecurity of accepting immigrants to Canada from war-affected countries.[2]

One further example demonstrates how the Canadian government, determined to be tough on terrorism after 2006, declared Tamils arriving by boat as threats even before they had landed in Canada. Comprehensive security checks are applied to all newcomers, whether asylum seekers or highly skilled economic immigrants. Yet, the geopolitical imaginations of some government officials cast aspersions on diaspora newcomers, especially those who arrived by boat. In October 2009, a ship carrying six dozen Tamil asylum seekers landed off of British Columbia's west coast. In August 2010, a second ship carrying 492 asylum seekers arrived in BC. Before the second ship arrived, *The Guardian* (2010a) reported that Canada's Public Safety Minister "had concerns that there may be members of the rebel Liberation Tigers of Tamil Eelam, or Tamil Tigers, on board." Lorne Waldman, a lawyer representing more than 50 of those asylum seekers, later told *The Guardian* that before the boat landed the tone was set. "From the get-go, it was suggested that there were criminals and terrorists aboard ... The Sri Lankan government has a huge interest in portraying them this way rather than as victims of a genocidal civil war. Some of those on board are victims of torture and have shrapnel wounds" (*The*

Guardian 2010b). A decade later, only one person has been convicted of smuggling offences. Janet Dench, executive director of the Canadian Council for Refugees commented,

> The government has spent years and huge amounts of money to fight the passengers of the Ocean Lady and the Sun Sea – in the courts, in the refugee hearing processes, detaining them as long as they could. All for what? ... The charges of criminality and security risks have been shown to be without foundation ... At least we can take pride in the fact that Canadian institutions and courts continue to treat people fairly (Dench cited in Quan 2017).[3]

We now move to the post-boat arrival, post-war moment in which our research was conducted in the Greater Toronto Area (GTA).

A Note on Research Methods

We employed two qualitative methods: four focus groups, convened in 2012, and 52 semi-structured interviews, held in 2013. All authors participated in conducting the research, with the first two authors convening the focus groups, and all of the authors conducting interviews. Focus groups were composed of five to six individuals and consisted of adult youth who were members of Tamil Student Associations (TSAs) at universities, and members of Tamil diaspora organisations with more diverse age profiles. The semi-structured interviews were conducted with both first- and second- generation Sri Lankan Tamil Canadians in Greater Toronto, extending to parts of southwestern Ontario. Interviews were held in English or Tamil, depending on participants' preferences. The interviews were coded using N-VIVO software by the third author. While formal interviews have not been conducted since 2013, the authors have returned to Sri Lanka in the interim and stayed abreast of scholarship and politics in the Tamil diaspora in Canada and beyond (c. f. Kandasamy 2019).

The sampling strategy employed was purposive in that we sought to recruit similar numbers of men and women, both immigrants from Sri Lanka (who arrived as adults and children) and Tamils born in Canada. Advertisements were placed in Tamil community online newspapers, health outreach listservs that focused on Tamil-speaking clientele, and on social media sites, such as those of Tamil Student Associations from all of the universities in Southwestern Ontario. Some snowball sampling was used when research participants suggested individuals from their social networks to participate in the study where additional representation was needed.

An interview guide was developed based on findings from the pilot phase of the study which included focus groups with Tamil-Canadian youth in the Greater Toronto Area. Interviews were conducted with 24 first-generation Tamils who immigrated to Canada, eight second-generation participants born in Canada for whom at least one parent was Tamil-identified, and twenty 1.5-generation participants who arrived in Canada as children, mostly in

Greater Toronto, but also in the Southern Ontario cities of London, Windsor, and Waterloo. First generation Tamil-Canadians are defined as *adults* who emigrated from Sri Lanka after the age of 13. The mean age of this group was 49 years, with an average age of arrival of 30 years. This group was also well-educated with all participants reporting that they had completed at least a high school diploma; 79% of this group had obtained a university degree or higher (highest level of education obtained: 29% graduate degree, 50% university degree, 16% some post-secondary education, and 4% high school diploma). The so-called '1.5-generation' Tamil-Canadians were those that emigrated from Sri Lanka prior to the age of 13 and were on average 28 years old at the time of the interviews. For this group, the average age of arrival in Canada was 6 years. This group was also well educated, with 75% of the group holding a university degree or graduate degree. Finally, second-generation Tamil-Canadians are those born in Canada. This group had a mean age of 23 years and were also a well-educated group: 12.5% had a graduate degree; 50% overall had a university degree.

Findings from the Tamil Diaspora

For this paper, we draw principally on responses from two N-VIVO codes from the transcripts, specifically 'Tamil nationalism in Canada' and 'LTTE – opinion of'. Recall the context of these interviews in the Canadian Tamil diaspora: the LTTE had been defeated in Sri Lanka, and the leader killed, by the Sri Lankan military. Some 40,000 Tamil civilians were also killed in the final throes of conflict, after international NGOs and UN agencies were asked to leave the Vanni region in Northern Sri Lanka. No independent national or international human rights inquiry was held to account for the final events of the war, including the disappearance of Tamils who surrendered. We provide as wide a range of responses here as found in the data. One second generation man, born in Canada, explained his relation to Tamil nationalism:

> the Tamil struggle has to move beyond the Tamil militancy ... including the Tamil Tiger flag. We don't have to carry around the Tamil Tiger flag to say we are for the human rights, or build a nation. It's not going to happen. And also, the thing is Canada is a very different country. They don't respect guns and all that ... So it's a much more mellow country so you have to be mellow and you cannot just have a flag with bullets (interview 220).

This sentiment of changing political views to adapt to a Canadian context was common among many respondents when asked their opinion of the LTTE, a question that is still a sensitive one within Tamil Canadian circles. One man of Tamil background born in Canada explained,

> [W]hen I was a kid and I was more naïve. I used to trust all the propaganda that I read, and a lot of the things I heard from my parents were for the LTTE. But as I got to be a bit older, and to be more objective about understanding what was happening, and reading from unbiased news sources, I realised that the LTTE was just as bad as the army and the

> government in certain ways. So I just felt like I couldn't really support their ambitions ... I don't really agree with their tactics. I mean I understand, I sympathise with their motives. I mean I think Tamils have been discriminated against for a very long time, the riots that happened, and there was a lot of horrible stuff that was happening, but the LTTE at times were just as bad as SL government in committing atrocities. ... I don't agree with child soldiers, or abducting underage children into the armed forces (interview 228).

The nuances between different expressions of Tamil nationalism, and differences across generations, are evident. We noticed that several of our respondents were able to separate, in their minds, the *reason* for the militant response in the first place and the ways in which the militant movement progressed throughout the war. In other words, the fact that the LTTE committed its own atrocities in no way nullified the legitimate militant response to decades of Sri Lankan government-backed violence in the first place. One Tamil man born in Sri Lanka noted, "I'm not a supporter of the LTTE, but [we need] somebody to, you know, say about our people, the Tamils. There should be somebody. Now there's nobody; people are suffering" (Interview 106). With the LTTE officially defeated by the Sri Lankan Government in 2009, Tamils are currently represented in Parliament by sixteen elected MPs who are part of the Tamil National Alliance (TNA).

Members of families we canvassed were often divided in their support for the LTTE. One second generation man was asked about the LTTE and whether his take on the organisation had changed over time:

> My feelings on the LTTE generally haven't changed. I was not a Tiger supporter. My dad generally felt that, you know, the things they did weren't good. And he didn't like the fact that they would extort money back. He felt, like a lot of other people, that they were the only people who dared fight back. And so for that they, he wouldn't put it this way, but this is the way I read it. That they could be excused for some of the things that they did. I definitely did not feel that way. I have a lot more problems with that idea. And generally I feel that they [f#$%*] Tamils over at the end of the war, with the things that they did. Just holding people back, and so on and so on. You know, not negotiating. I mean they had a chance at the very, very end to negotiate (interview 216).

His father's conditional support of the LTTE appears quite distinct from his son's in this case. References to parents' views of the LTTE came up often. One Tamil man born in Sri Lanka recounted the vast variations in political positions among Tamils, from federalists who believed in Tamil autonomy within Sri Lanka, and separatists who were willing to fight for a separate state of Tamil Eelam.

> So currently there's most of the moderate groups, they support the elected parliamentarians, the Tamil parliamentarians in SL, and they want them to take charge and march forward with the issues. Right? Whereas the extreme group, they don't respect them. They still want to go through the other way of, eventually, they don't openly say to take arms again, but I think that's in the back of their mind. Basically because they can't say that openly in Canada ... I felt strongly about them [LTTE] because like I said, without them I wouldn't be here right now. And at the end of the day, not everything they did was good. But they had to do what they had to do ... That's why I like the way my dad

approached it, like you have to look at both sides, and at the end of the day, the LTTE did do a lot of bad as well, but at the end of the day, you have to realise that at a time when we were being exploited and we were being discriminated against there was no one standing up for us (interview 103).

A woman of Tamil background born in Canada recounted tension within her own family and the contested positions of her parents on the matter:

> So, in our house it's controversial, because my dad is very pro LTTE, while my mom is very, she thinks that like regardless, whichever side it is, they killed people on both sides. So, it's still, it's wrong regardless of whether who does it, but obviously the Sinhalese government has done worse injustice than the LTTE. So it always like, I was always critical of that. Yes, I would say yes I support an organisation that supports the cause of the Tamils, but obviously you have to be critical of what they did in their past too (interview 231).

Departing from the majority position in her own family, another woman of Tamil background born in Canada expressed critique of the Tigers and their Hero's Day (*Maveerar Naal*) to remember fallen cadres of the LTTE:

> [She sighs] Both my parents' families have people that were killed – they were part of the LTTE and they were killed. So the whole argument is "ohh you're a traitor!" [because she refuses to attend Maveerar Naal]. No. I have family members that have been in the LTTE and died in battle, whatever. But for all the reasons I've spoken to about, I will never ever go to a Maveerar Naal, no. So racist and like ugh [sounds of disgust]. Yea so problematic on so many levels.

[Interviewer asks, what do you mean in terms of it being racist?]

> Like Maveerar Naal is this important supporting of Jaffna Tamils and their support of the LTTE. It's a very racist politics against Muslims like, it's very racist. Like only certain people are allowed to come to this, right? Again, the LTTE forcibly expelled 150,000 Muslim communities that were a very important part of Tamil people's lives. Nobody talks about that. Really, like supporting that group is saying, automatically you're saying I support every action that they've done, right? Like saying oh my heroes. No they are not heroes! They've been pivotal in breaking up Tamil communities. So when you celebrate this group, you are automatically saying I support the discrimination of Muslim communities. No, that is very racist. Islamophobic and racist (interview 225).

This historicised view of the LTTE and its 1990 ethnic cleansing of Muslims from the Northern and Northeastern parts of Sri Lanka (Thiranagama 2011) where they spoke Tamil and lived peacefully with Tamils interrupts the separatist project and challenges the authority of the LTTE. Put another way in a subsequent interview with a second-generation woman of Tamil background, "I don't know. ... I think why generally it's so complicated to be a Tamil-Canadian is because can you be Tamil and not support LTTE? Yea I think you can, but it's such a complicated feeling" (Interview 227).

Certainly, the experience of Tamil nationalism and the idea of militancy in the diaspora among those born in Canada is complicated by the indirect experience of violence, loss, and competing ethnonationalist politics, yet some of those who came to Canada express a change from their earlier views of the LTTE. As one Tamil woman originally from Sri Lanka commented:

> I don't know. I have no comment. You know, at one time when it started we thought it's good because it's going to a good cause, like equal rights and all those things. But when it happened, and it went on a wrong route, like killing their own, the other groups started killing everybody ... Both [the Sri Lankan Government and LTTE] are doing the wrong things (interview 119).

All of these passages focus on the politics of Sri Lanka in Canada, not on politics in Canada. Everyone interviewed was based in Canada at the time of the interviews. One Tamil woman who came to Canada from Sri Lanka was asked about her thoughts on the LTTE and whether it had a negative effect in Canada; instead she was critical of the Canadian Government:

> Negativity was done in the Conservative government ... putting the ban on Tamil people. You know. The political ban. So that rest of the time it was, 'cause it was really easy for the Sri Lankan government to tell that they are terrorists. Right? So it's a freedom struggle. It's a struggle of one ethnic group. And then they name that as terrorism. So they not really, so if the sister, or some, what they did to the Aboriginal people here it was not terrorism. So they really had, you know, they accepted refugees, Tamils as refugees, but why couldn't they accept the cause behind the refugees? (interview 115).

While space limitations do not permit us to elaborate, a number of respondents expressed their disappointment, frustration and anger with the Canadian Government for doing nothing as Tamil civilians were being killed in the spring of 2009. Pan-Canadian petitions were signed; letters to elected government representatives were written. Research participants' criticisms were that Canada did not stand up for Tamil human rights and basic protection from slaughter at the hands of the Sri Lankan military. There was no evidence in our sample of negativity towards Canadians or civil society organisations.

In order to validate our data and consolidate the finding that there were no negative sentiments towards Canadian civil society in our sample, we turn to a database that aggregates findings of extremism in Canada based on public data. In it there is no evidence of LTTE actions or extremism causing random injury or death in Canada; however, a few examples of harm to Tamils living in Canada have been recorded in a few incidents (CID 2019). For example, a critic of the LTTE, journalist D.B.S. Jeyeraj, did face a beating in the 1990s for his published views. Those who faced extortion and threats on Canadian soil were mostly likely to be Tamil and are not officially recorded. Every Tamil who could was expected to support the 'Tamil cause' represented by the LTTE until its defeat in Sri Lanka in 2009 (Amarasingam 2015). In many ways our research, conducted more than three years after the end of the war, was possible because the LTTE control of Tamils in the Canadian diaspora had loosened dramatically.

Elsewhere, we have argued that Tamils in Greater Toronto have both diasporic affiliations and Canadian ones. Canada, not Sri Lanka, is home to almost all of our respondents. Not uncritically, many respondents saw multiculturalism in another paper less as state policy than as a *practice* that created space for belonging where none existed for Tamils in Sri Lanka (Amarasingam et al. 2015). A 75-year-old Tamil man who arrived in Canada at the age of 45 (Interview 105) had migrated from Sri Lanka at the age of 25 in 1962, going to the United Kingdom to study, and remained there for twenty years before arriving in Canada. In asking if he would like to return, he said, 'In Sri Lanka, you're not respected as a Tamil,' he noted, 'you feel that you are one below, you know? In Canada, you feel like you can give your life for this country because you are 100% like anybody else. In Sri Lanka, you are not 100% like the rest of the majority.' Life in the UK also emerged as an important point of comparison to Canada: 'The UK is not an immigrant country,' he argued, 'so you are never a part of the country. You're always an immigrant. In Canada, everyone is an immigrant. So, Canada can be your home.' Diaspora affiliations combine with Canadian ones. These sentiments belie a diaspora geopolitics of belonging, where exiled Tamils feel more at home in one reception context than another.

Conclusion

Tamil nationalisms are alive and well in the Greater Toronto diaspora, yet views about them and the LTTE specifically by diaspora subjects vary tremendously. The analysis of excerpts about the nuanced sense of Tamil nationalism in Canada presented here is part of diaspora geopolitics: a quotidian geopolitics of protest and survival framed by some historical allegiances to a militant separatist guerilla group ostensibly fighting for Tamils, but also strongly influenced by the liberal democratic asylum policies and practices that accepted these diasporic subjects as Canadians in the first instance. The shared histories of violence and transnational displacement among people now living on safer ground constitute a site and subject of diaspora geopolitics. Nationalism stemming from conflict, exclusion, and discrimination can be traced back to independence in 1948, to the Sinhala-only Act of 1956, to the anti-Tamil pogroms in Sri Lanka in 1983, and most recently to the widespread violence, killing, and internment of Tamils in the country with impunity in 2009 (ICG 2017).

Likewise, people's views of the separatist and militant LTTE vary tremendously, even *within* given families in the Tamil diaspora. Despite the military defeat of the LTTE in Sri Lanka, Tamil nationalism in the Canadian diaspora is a proxy for 'Tamilness' – a diaspora geopolitics of shared histories of violence and displacement being enacted in a new neighbourhood, namely Greater Toronto. We have shown above that this politics-at-a-distance in Canada creates a distinct kind of Tamil nationalism, one that is outraged by the war crimes of the Sri Lankan state but also wary of the LTTE complicities in violence against unarmed Tamil people. By redirecting state-centric concerns that envisage diaspora newcomers as sources of extremism, this paper has used diaspora geopolitics to foreground different histories of violence, displacement, and security at ground level – in the living rooms, classrooms, and coffee shops where we interviewed Tamils living in Canada. Their connections to and concern for Tamils still living in Sri Lanka in the aftermath of mass killings and the impunity continue as they make sense of both personal experiences and geopolitical forces that bear down upon them.

A cautionary note for researchers in this field of diaspora geopolitics is important. Our research finds little, if any, evidence to fuel a geopolitical imagination that links diasporas from war zones – like Tamils from Sri Lanka living in Canada – with extremist violence.[4] Research that asks whether such new Canadians 'import conflict' with them when they immigrate to Canada is a leading question that generates a violence of its own, casting racialised newcomers as potential threats (Monahan, Berns-McGown, and Morden 2014). Yet, Monahan et al.'s *own* interview findings dispel the opinions collected from the telephone survey that found that 57% of respondents felt newcomers from war zones import conflict. To cast aspersions on racialised newcomers from war-affected countries *by implying that they are a risk* in a phone survey question is potentially a form of violence *against* diasporas. An emphasis in diaspora geopolitics, then, is its refusal of state securitisation practices targeted at racialized newcomers from war-affected countries.

In Canada, our data show that the human rights atrocities of 2009 in Sri Lanka stoked and solidified Tamil nationalism in Canada, uniting Tamils across the world in various countries through diaspora geopolitics, and perhaps *refugia* (Van Hear 2017). Tamil nationalism in Canada has never been directed *against* the Canadian state or civil society. To the contrary, and as we have shown elsewhere, it has galvanised a sense of belonging to Canada among members of the Tamil diaspora in the Greater Toronto Area (Amarasingam, Naganathan, and Hyndman 2016; Whitaker 2016). Official acceptance rates of asylum seekers from Sri Lanka remain high (Rehaag 2019).

Tamil Canadians have a broad range of views about the LTTE. Many were critical of its violent tactics, but saw it as the sole organisation championing the human rights of Tamils when the Canadian Government did little to interrupt or stop the violence against ordinary people in Sri Lanka, pointing to the tension between the LTTE as a militant, separatist group and as champion and protector of Tamils when they were the targets of brutal violence and human right atrocities. The massacre of thousands of Tamil civilians in Mullivaikkal in the last months and weeks of the military conflict, largely by the Sri Lankan military, also revealed that the Tigers used civilians as human shields (Weiss 2012; Whitaker 2016). What is more egregious is that the world's biggest democracies and defenders of human rights watched this deadly military operation proceed after international organisations were asked to leave the region. With no more witnesses to monitor violence and war crimes, deadly transgressions of humanitarian law and human rights were rolled out with impunity and fatal consequences while members of the Tamil diaspora vehemently protested to no avail from afar.

Notes

1. Canadian history includes one dramatic exception to the 'peaceful diaspora' pattern: the bombing of Air India Flight 182 en route from Montreal to London (with a connection to Delhi) in June 1985 on which 329 people perished just off the coast of Ireland. The attack was Canada's most fatal terrorist incident, with a majority of the passengers being Canadian citizens. The 2010 Air India Inquiry report stated that Canadian authorities failed to effectively investigate the bombing at the time; only in 2005 did the government initiate an official commission of inquiry into Flight 182 (Singh 2015). The attack was traced to Sikh extremists living in Canada; one manslaughter conviction was made. On January 8, 2020, Ukraine International Airlines Flight 752, flying from Tehran to Kiev, was shot down shortly after take-off. The Iranian Government admitted to mistakenly firing two missiles at the passenger plane, killing 176 people, 63 of whom were Canadians; many more had permanent residence or international student status in Canada. Yet this was an attack *by* the state on civilians, so does not represent violent extremism except by Iranian authorities, and is likely related to the US attack and killing of Major-General Qassim Suleimani, Commander of the Iranian Forces the same week.
2. More than twenty-five years after the Air India bombing, the Canadian Government funded the Kanishka Project, a counter-terrorism initiative which aimed to identify and combat extremism through research, outreach, and related activities (Public Safety Canada 2018). The Kanishka Project, named after the downed Air India plane in 1985, 'Emperor Kanishka', was implemented during the tenure of Prime Minister Stephen Harper's Conservative majority government from 2011–15 (Public Safety Canada 2018b). In this brief note we outline one study commissioned funded by the Government through the Kanishka Project as a point of departure for the original findings and data we collected section of the paper. The study, entitled "The Perception and Reality of "Imported Conflict" in Canada" was an initiative established to better understand terrorism in Canadian society (Monahan, Berns-McGown, and Morden 2014). The study employed two main methods, which generated contradictory findings. A random telephone survey was conducted with 4500 Canadians who were asked if they thought that members of diasporas who immigrate to Canada from conflict zones 'import conflict'. This is a leading question and a loaded one in terms of survey design. The very act of asking 4500 people this question could be considered a mode of securitising immigrants to Canada, that is, creating a group of highly racialised newcomers as a threat to Canadian society. To plant such an idea in the minds of unsuspecting respondents who may know little about the topic is prejudicial. Some 57% of respondents to this leading question replied in the affirmative. We are concerned that the study *securitises* the very people who come to Canada from countries affected by war, human rights atrocities, and other conditions of persecution – that is to say, the question about whether they 'import conflict' renders

them as threats. In contrast to this leading and potentially xenophobic line of questioning, 220 face-to-face interviews and twelve focus groups were conducted with first and second-generation diaspora members, including with a number of Tamil and Sinhalese young people from Sri Lanka. The findings from the interviews were consistent and provided quite the opposite findings: people who immigrate to Canada from war zones come to escape violence and enjoy the rights and freedoms, as well as laws and responsibilities, of life in Canada (Monahan, Berns-McGown, and Morden 2014). Members of these communities of Canadians who come from conflict unequivocally repudiate violence in Canada as a response to, or means of resolving, overseas conflict (Monahan, Berns-McGown, and Morden 2014, 10). Among Tamils consulted, their views of the Tigers were diverse (ibid: 91): "Tamil respondents had differing views of the Tigers. Some were strongly supportive of the group and argued that they had defended the Tamil people with integrity. Others disapproved of many of the tactics employed by the Tigers, but maintain that they were the only presence on the island with the capacity and willingness to protect Tamil citizens against the Sri Lankan state. Still others revile the Tigers, and shared deeply troubling personal stories about violence visited on their families by the Tigers because of political dissent." Many Tamils added that " ... education is the primary tool of choice to contest the conflict in the future." There is no armed struggle. That is universally understood. But when the young people wave the LTTE flag it does not stand for armed struggle. It is the sense of Tamil identity that they need. PTSD will intensify if it is not addressed. And these young people have all suffered from racism here – and that exacerbates the pain. The conversation has shifted. It used to be about defeating the rebels but that was accomplished and now it is about destroying our culture completely. *(P., Tamil woman, 34, b. Killinochchi, to Canada at 16)* There is no *physical violence*: the community values education and *being involved in criminal activity has a stigma attached*. The focus is on upward mobility. People just shut down and don't engage with Sinhalese. But we are in a lull. How long will it last? Are we waiting to see if the Sri Lankan government does anything different? Will there be a post-lull reaction? *(T., Tamil woman, 23, b. Colombo, to Canada at 6; italics added) Being Canadian means being away from that brutality and violence ... Why hate the Sinhalese people? They are just people too. What is the point?* That is the trouble. Sinhalese people have been affected as well. *(N., Tamil woman, 30, b. eastern province, to Canada at 10: italics added).* The common element of all my friends is that being Canadian is very important to us. Our shared recognition of being Canadian gives us the ground to build on. (V., Sinhalese man, 29, b. Colombo, to Canada at 16). These excerpts from the interviews are important correctives and evidence illustrative of the ways in which actual people living in the Tamil diaspora think about violence, inter-ethnic conflict, and living in Canada. They represent a wide range of views – both supportive and critical of the Tamil Tigers. The authors' observation, based on their findings from the interviews, is that diaspora newcomers to Canada do not 'import conflict' as the grey literature contends in its telephone survey. Recall that 57% of respondents responded affirmatively to a leading question about whether newcomers from war zones import conflict when they immigrate to Canada (Monahan, Berns-McGown, and Morden 2014).

3. From the 2009 ship, the Ocean Lady, eight people were deemed inadmissible and received deportation orders, 36 refugee claims were accepted, and 21 claims were rejected. In the MV Sun Sea cases, 22 were ordered deported after being found inadmissible, 230 refugee claims were accepted and 107 claims were rejected. Many claims remain in appeal.

4. One source links the death of a diplomat to one diaspora in Canada: Armenian militants attacked the Turkish Embassy in Ottawa in 1982, killing its military attaché on his way to work (CID 2019).

Acknowledgments

The authors would like to thank the Social Sciences and Humanities Research Council of Canada for funding this research.

References

Abraham, I. 2015. How India became territorial: Foreign policy, diaspora, geopolitics. *International Affairs* 91 (4):915–16. doi:10.1111/1468-2346.12377.

Amarasingam, A. 2015. *Pain, pride, and politics: Social movement activism and the Sri Lankan tamil diaspora in Canada*. Athens: University of Georgia Press.

Amarasingam, A. 2016. Post-war Sri Lanka and the "big bad" diaspora. In *Sri Lanka: The struggle for peace in the aftermath of war*, ed. A. Amarasingam and D. Bass, 201–19. London: Hurst and Co.

Amarasingam, A., G. Naganathan, and J. Hyndman. 2016. Canadian multiculturalism as banal nationalism. *Canadian Ethnic Studies* 48 (2):119–42. doi:10.1353/ces.2016.0016.

Ashutosh, I. 2013. Immigrant protests in Toronto: Diaspora and Sri Lanka's civil war. *Citizenship Studies* 17 (2):197–210.

BBC. 2012. Sri Lanka closes huge Menik farm displacement camps. 24 September. https://www.bbc.com/news/world-asia-19703826

Bell, S. 2000. Sri Lanka's civil war and the Canadian connection, *The National Post* June 3.

Bell, S. 2001. Ottawa won't renew funding for Tamil society, *The National Post* December 3.

Carter, S. 2005. The geopolitics of diaspora. *Area* 37 (1):54–63. doi:10.1111/j.1475-4762.2005.00601.x.

CBC [Canadian Broadcasting Corporation]. 2006. Canada adds Tamil Tigers to list of terrorist groups. *CBC news*, April 10 http://www.cbc.ca/news/canada/canada-adds-tamil-tigers-to-list-of-terrorist-groups-1.603477.

CBC [Canadian Broadcasting Corporation]. 2008. Canada lists world Tamil movement as terrorist organization. June 16 http://www.cbc.ca/news/canada/canada-lists-world-tamil-movement-as-terrorist-organization-1.707040.

CBC [Canadian Broadcasting Corporation]. 2009a. More than 30,000 Tamil supporters descend on Parliament Hill, April 21. https://www.cbc.ca/news/canada/ottawa/more-than-30-000-tamil-supporters-descend-on-parliament-hill-1.793949

CBC [Canadian Broadcasting Corporation]. 2009b. Tamil protester end blockade on major Toronto highway. https://www.cbc.ca/news/canada/toronto/tamil-protesters-end-blockade-on-major-toronto-highway-1.829118.

CID [Canadian Incident Database]. 2019. TSAS. http://extremism.ca/.

Cresswell, T. 2006. *On the move: Mobility in the modern Western world*. London: Routledge.

Crosby, A., and M. B. Lykes. 2019. *Beyond repair?: Mayan women's protagonism in the aftermath of genocidal harm*. New Brunswick: Rutgers University Press.

De Genova, N. 2017. Introduction: The borders of "Europe" and the European question. In *The borders of "Europe": Autonomy of migration, tactics of bordering*, ed. N. De Genova, 1–36. Durham, NC: Duke University Press.

Fuglerud, O. 1999. *Life on the outside: The Tamil diaspora and long distance nationalism*. London: Pluto Press.

Guardian. 2010a. Canadian navy boards ship carrying Tamil migrants from Sri Lanka. August 13. https://www.theguardian.com/world/2010/aug/13/canada-vessel-tamil-migrants-sri-lanka.

Guardian. 2010b. Sri Lankan Tamil refugees spark racism row in Canada. September 7. https://www.theguardian.com/world/2010/sep/07/canada-tamil-refugees-racism-debate.

Harrison, F. 2012. *Still counting the dead: Stories from Sri Lanka's killing fields*. London: Portobello Books.

Haviland, C. 2012. Sri Lanka government publishes war death toll statistics. *BBC*, February 24. https://www.bbc.com/news/world-asia-17156686

Human Rights Watch. 2010. Sri Lanka: Events of 2009. https://www.hrw.org/world-report/2010/country-chapters/sri-lanka

Hunter, P. 2016. Tamil protester looks back at Gardiner takeover with mixed feelings. *The Toronto Star*, May 9. https://www.thestar.com/news/insight/2016/05/09/tamil-protester-looks-back-at-gardiner-takeover-with-mixed-feelings.html

Hyndman, J. 2003. Aid, conflict, and migration: The Canada-Sri Lanka connection. *The Canadian Geographer* 47 (3):251–68. doi:10.1111/1541-0064.00021.

Hyndman, J., and A. Mountz. 2007. Refuge or refusal: Geography of exclusion. In *Violent geographies*, ed. D. Gregory and A. Pred, 77–92. New York: Routledge.

Hyndman, J. 2010. Introduction: The feminist politics of refugee migration. *Gender, Place and Culture (Special Issue Editor)* 17 (4):453–59. http://jhyndman.info.yorku.ca/files/2017/01/Introduction.pdf.

Hyndman, J. 2013a. To move or not to move: Im/mobility in Sri Lanka's war without sound. Invited presentation at *Mobilities: Immobilities Workshop*, Bergen, Norway, September 6–7.

Hyndman, J. 2013b. To move or not to move: Im/mobility in Sri Lanka's war without sound, Invited talk at Mobilities: Immobilities Workshop, University of Bergen, Norway, September 6–7.

Hyndman, J., and W. Giles. 2011. Waiting for what? The feminization of asylum in protracted situations. *Gender, Place, and Culture* 18 (3):361–79. doi:10.1080/0966369X.2011.566347.

International Crisis Group. 2010. War crimes in Sri Lanka. Report 191 Asia, May 17th, ICG website. Accessed October 8, 2019. https://www.crisisgroup.org/asia/south-asia/sri-lanka/war-crimes-sri-lanka.

International Crisis Group. 2017. Transition to nowhere. Report 286 Asia, May 16th, ICG website. Accessed October 8, 2019. https://www.crisisgroup.org/asia/south-asia/sri-lanka/286-sri-lanka-s-transition-nowhere.

International Crisis Group. 2020. Sri Lanka [Country Report]. Accessed March 7, 2020. https://www.crisisgroup.org/asia/south-asia/sri-lanka.

Jones, R. 2016. *Violent borders: Refugees and the right to move*. New York: Verso.

Kandasamy, N. 2019. The craft of belonging: Exploring the resettlement experiences of young Tamil survivors of Sri Lanka's civil war in Australia, PhD Dissertation, University of Melbourne ORCHID ID 0000-0002-5904-8223.

Lynch, C. 2011. U.N.: Sri Lanka's crushing of Tamil Tigers may have killed 40,000 civilians. *Washington Post*, April 21. https://www.washingtonpost.com/world/un-sri-lankas-crushing-of-tamil-tigers-may-have-killed-40000civilians/2011/04/21/AFU14hJE_story.html?noredirect=on&utm_term=.0dc800b8024a.

Malkki, L. 1996. Speechless emissaries: Refugees, humanitarianism, and dehistoricization. *Cultural Anthropology* 11 (3):377–404. doi:10.1525/can.1996.11.3.02a00050.

Massey, D. 1991. A global sense of place. *Marxism Today* 24–29.

Mayer, T. 2004. Embodied nationalisms. In *Mapping women, making politics*, ed. L. Staeheli, E. Kofman, and L. Peake, 153–68.

McDowell, C. 1996. *A Tamil asylum diaspora: Sri Lankan migration, settlement and politics in Switzerland*. New York/Oxford: Berghahn Books.

McNeely, A., and S. Lough. 2014. Which countries do Canadian immigrants come from? *Capital News.* https://capitalnews.ca/coming-to-canada/project/coming-going/.

Merriam-Webster. 2019. Disaspora. https://www.merriam-webster.com/dictionary/diaspora.

Monahan, J., R. Berns-McGown, and M. Morden. 2014. The perception and reality of "Imported conflict" in Canada. Ottawa: The Mosaic Institute. http://media.wix.com/ugd/102a59_fed15d58a7ed4705ae1ec35221b38732.pdf.

Mountz, A., and N. Hiemstra. 2014. Chaos and crisis: Dissecting the spatiotemporal logics of contemporary migrations and state practices. *Annals of the Association of American Geographers* 104 (2):382–90. doi:10.1080/00045608.2013.857547.

Pain, R., and S. J. Smith. 2008. *Fear: Critical geopolitics and everyday life.* Farnham: Ashgate.

Public Safety Canada. 2018a. Building resilience against terrorism: Canada's counter-terrorism strategy. https://www.publicsafety.gc.ca/cnt/rsrcs/pblctns/rslnc-gnst-trrrsm/index-en.aspx.

Public Safety Canada. 2018b. Kanishka project. https://www.publicsafety.gc.ca/cnt/ntnl-scrt/cntr-trrrsm/r-nd-flght-182/knshk/index-en.aspx.

Quan, D. 2017. Years after two ships brought 568 migrants to Canada, seven acquittals and one conviction. *The National Post.* https://nationalpost.com/news/canada/years-after-two-ships-brought-568-migrants-to-canada-seven-acquittals-and-one-conviction

Rehaag, S. (2019)"2018 Refugee Claim Data and IRB Member Recognition Rates" (19 June). Accessed 22 Sept 2020 at https://ccrweb.ca/en/2018-refugee-claim-data

Riga, A. 2018. Inside the life of Quebec mosque killer Alexandre Bissonette. *Montreal Gazette*, April 23. https://montrealgazette.com/news/local-news/alexandre-bissonnette-inside-the-life-of-a-mass-murderer

Sharp, J. P. 2011. "Subaltern geopolitics: Introduction", editorial. *Geoforum* 42 (3):271–73. doi:10.1016/j.geoforum.2011.04.006.

Sharp, J. P. 2019. Practising subalternity? Nyerere's Tanzania, the Dar School and postcolonial geopolitical imagination. In *Subaltern geographies*, ed. T. Jazeel and S. Legg. Athens GA: University of Georgia Press.

Sheller, M., and J. Urry. 2006. The new mobilities paradigm. *Environment & Planning A* 38:207–26. doi:10.1068/a37268.

Shohat, E. 2006. *Taboo memories, diasporic voices.* Durham NC: Duke UP.

Singh, M. 2015. The bombing of air India flight 182: Demanding justice, public inquiries, and acts of citizenship. PhD Dissertation, Dept. of Communications, Simon Fraser University.

Sriskandarajah, D. 2005. Tamil diaspora politics. In *Encyclopedia of diasporas*, ed. M. Ember, C. R. Ember, and I. Skoggard, 492-498. Boston, MA: Springer.

Van Hear, N. 2005. Refugee diasporas or refugees in diaspora. In *Encyclopedia of diasporas*, ed. M. Ember, C. R. Ember, and I. Skoggard, 580-591. Boston, MA: Springer.

Van Hear, N. 2017. Imagining refugia: Could a new transnational polity help solve the refugee crisis. *Foreign Affairs Newsletter*, October 17. https://www.foreignaffairs.com/articles/world/2017-10-17/imagining-refugia.

Van Hear, N., V. Barbelet, C. Bennett, and H. A. Lutz. 2018. Imagining refugia: Thinking outside the current refugee regime. *Migration and Society: Advances in Research* 1:175–94. doi:10.3167/arms.2018.010116.

Weiss, G. 2012. *The cage: The fight for Sri Lanka and the last days of the Tamil tigers.* New York: Bellevue Literary Press.

Whitaker, M. 2016. "What can we say?" Some preliminary thoughts regarding the epistemology of feeling and saying among Tamils in post-war Sri Lanka and in the diaspora. In *Sri Lanka: The struggle for peace in the aftermath of war*, ed. A. Amarasingam and D. Bass, 181–200. London: Hurst and Co.

Geopoliticizing Geographies of Care: Scales of Responsibility Towards Sea-borne Migrants and Refugees in the Mediterranean

Sara McDowell

ABSTRACT
Each year thousands of people seeking better lives in Europe make the treacherous journey across the Mediterranean. Many of those struggling or stranded at sea are rescued by 'boat people' comprising NGOs, humanitarian organizations, coast guards and merchant vessels. Under maritime law there is a duty of care towards anyone that experiences difficulty at sea. There is, too, a duty of care by States who under the same law are required to assist ships and allow the disembarkation of those in danger. Yet this practice has important legal, ethical and practical implications and has been challenged by right-leaning political regimes who, making good on election promises to ease immigration, have prohibited such vessels to dock at their ports. This paper, using a case study approach of the humanitarian vessel the Aquarius, considers the ways in which the geographies of care intersect and collide with the geopolitical framing of migrants and refugees. In doing so the paper makes two important contributions. First, it extends conceptualizations of care geographies which are more typically applied to the spatial outworking of health and wellbeing to European migration. It thinks about how care is administered, contested and politicized. The complex concept of care offers a rich lens through which to critique the framing of seaborne migrants and refugees in Europe. Through giving or circumventing legal responsibilities to provide care, seaborne migrants are either humanized or dehumanized. Second, through unpacking the legislative and ethical frameworks shaping search and rescue (SAR) activities in the Mediterranean, we can observe a distinct 'geopoliticizing of care and responsibility' whereby these individuals become pawns in wider power dynamics within the European Union.

Introduction

In June 2018, the Aquarius, an NGO vessel operating in the Mediterranean intercepted more than 600 sea-borne migrants in distress trying to make their way to the shores of Europe (Wintour, Tondo, and Kirchgaessar 2018). It sailed to the nearest port in Italy, only to be refused entry by the new Italian

Minister of Interior who had been in post only a matter of weeks. The ship set sail for Malta, having been turned away from Italy, only to once again be refused entry. Aquarius was eventually welcomed to dock in the Port of Valencia in Spain almost three weeks later, yet not before unleashing a particularly fractious and heated geopolitical debate about modes of care and responsibility towards those seeking refuge in Europe. While scholars such as Hyndman and Mountz (2008) have investigated the legal responsibilities States have towards migrants and those seeking refuge, we rarely think about migration within the context of giving (or circumventing) care. Migrants and refugees are not, of course, without agency and power as Mainwaring (2016) suggests, yet those who are seeking protection or simply a better life often find themselves bound up in care geographies. That care is contingent, I suggest, on an array of interconnected yet complex, moral, ethical, legal and geopolitical frameworks and practices.

The fate of thousands of seaborne migrants and refugees making the treacherous and often fatal journey across the Mediterranean each year (UNOCGA 2018) rests in part, on the actions of what Pugh (2004) refers to as 'boat people': those operating shipping or military vessels; NGOs and charities patrolling international waters, and State-operated search and rescue (henceforth SAR) vessels navigating complex legal and territorial jurisdictions. The fate of these people is influenced equally on the actions of individual States whose responsibility is dictated by international laws and supranational organizations (see DeBono 2013), or by their geography (or even controversially by their economic power-see, for example, Hyndman 2000). It is, too, shaped by public discourse which feeds into the actions of prominent and vocal politicians such as Italy's Matteo Salvini, who almost unilaterally decide whether a vessel carrying migrants or refugees should be allowed to dock. This is further complicated by the presence of smugglers and traffickers who have used the blurred boundaries of responsibility to carry people across the Mediterranean. Care within the context of migration is, I suggest, highly nuanced across time and place. The caregiving process may begin whenever a vessel saves or intercepts those in danger, but this care does not end when a ship docks at the nearest port. The future care of migrants and refugees is a difficult and sometimes fraught process.

Giving and receiving care as Fisher and Tonto attest (1990, 40), is a practice that individuals engage with to 'maintain, continue and repair our world so that we can live in it as well as possible'. Popke (2006) agrees, suggesting that it can instil a sense of responsibility not only towards those with whom we have some sort of emotional relationship, but also towards different and distinct others. He continues 'care is more than simply a social relation with moral and ethical dimensions: it can also be the basis for alternative ethical standpoints with implications for how we view traditional notions of citizenship and politics' (2006, 41). Care therefore can be viewed as being bound to the idea of citizenship and the right to belong. It is argued there that it is also inextricably linked to humanizing (and thus dehumanizing) behaviour.

The overarching aim of this paper is to think about the ways in which complex geographies of care, legal responsibility and responsibility under international law across varying scales intersect and collide with the geopolitical framing of migrants and refugees within Europe. On one level, this specific example of Aquarius with which the paper opens, reveals dichotomous efforts by multiple actors to engage in a practice and discourse that, in seeking to determine the extent of which they can or are willing to care for those in danger, contributes to the humanization and dehumanization of those very individuals. Dehumanizing practice according to Bleiker et al. (2013) is orchestrated by individuals or groups in society who want to protect their privileged positions. By perceiving refugees or migrants as different or undeserving of an equal status, they are stripped of their identity as human beings. On another, it speaks of a complex network of blurred legislative, territorial and humanitarian boundaries that complicate behaviours towards vulnerable individuals. In doing so this paper makes two important contributions. First, it extends conceptualizations of care geographies more typically applied to readings of health and wellbeing to European migration. It thinks about the ways in which care is administered, contested and politicized as individuals attempt to cross the Mediterranean Sea. Care, I suggest, offers a rich lens through which to critique the framing of migrants in Europe. Second, through unpacking the legislative and moral frameworks shaping SAR activities in the Mediterranean, we can observe a distinct 'geopoliticizing of care and responsibility' whereby migrants become pawns in wider power struggles within the European Union.

The paper uses a case study approach to examine the controversy surrounding NGO vessels and to tease out the power dynamics embedded within geographies of care that underpin the practice of making and unmaking refugees. The cases were selected following widespread public interest across Europe and a series of publicized high-profile exchanges between stakeholders. Data was collated through an analysis of policy and communication material pertaining to the vessels and their activities over the course of six months in 2018. Statements issued by politicians, NGOs, and European institutions were thematically analysed and coded. The text of legal frameworks shaping how actors across a multiplicity of scales could and should engage with sea-borne migrants was also analysed. In addition, media reports were mapped and examined using Carvalho's (2008) methodological approach which examines language, structure and surface descriptors. Social media platforms, unsurprisingly, produced a rich pool of qualitative data. Politicians, humanitarian organizations and the public used social media to engage in debates about the duty of care and responsibility and in doing so reframed the labels assigned to refugees and migrants. It should be noted that this paper is not attempting to present a pan-European presentation of the EU, rather it aims to demonstrate some of the nuanced regional approaches to care and responsibility within a complex geopolitical framework. Furthermore, it gives us a sense of some of the geopolitical wrangling taking place at a specific point in the migration 'crisis'.

The paper begins by introducing the conceptual framework, defining care and considering how it relates to the fields of mobility and migration. A scaled thematic discussion follows. It begins by looking at some of the legal frameworks that frame how States within the EU 'should' care for those who seek refuge and suggest that the 'unintended consequences' of legislation that is supposed to care for migrants can often serve to dehumanize them and remove their individuality (McDowell, Braniff., and Murphy 2017). It then discusses the role of humanitarian organizations before considering the role of individual States in this particular crisis, as well as high-profile politicians. The paper ends with a discussion on how public discourse that is framed within EU geopolitical power struggles can feed into and influence the decision of high-profile politicians who, making good on election promises, circumvent legal frameworks.

Conceptualizing Care within the Context of Migration

Care transcends socio-spatial boundaries (Popke 2006). Each of us engage in care geographies across multiple scales and times. For Lawson (2007) care is 'embedded in all of our encounters and interactions', even if it is not explicitly recognized. Often conceived as an embodied action (Hughes et al. 2005), definitions of care range from emotional responses towards something or someone in need, to the act of providing physical and/or psychological care towards a person or thing (see Conradson 2003). For Held (2006), care is not necessarily an activity, rather it is rooted in ideas about how we intersect and relate to others across multiple scales. This has important implications for migration policy and practice. How we view individuals who are seeking refuge or a better life, plays an important role in policymaking and the respective practices of those States, SAR vessels and humanitarian organizations who encounter sea-borne migrants and refugees as they move through contested and blurred borders.

Geographers have made a marked contribution to our understanding of the spaces (McKie, Gregory, and Bowlby 2002; Milligan and Wiles 2010) and outworking of care (Popke 2006), although this has not yet reached the complex domain of migration. Davidson and Milligan's (2004) conceptualization of the social dimensions of caring argue for a more nuanced reading of the effective and emotive implications of socially produced landscapes while Brown (cited in Popke 2006, 11) notes that questions of care 'cannot simply be mapped onto the existing liberal democratic maps of the political. They transform its very foundation'. The inexorable link between the social and political has also been the subject of Lawson's (2007) work. In reminding us that care 'ethics' is a social process and practice that is contextually shaped and influenced, she suggests it is intimately bound up in power dynamics and structures and therefore might be considered outside the domain of health geography. The marginalization of care in specific places and of specific people, she suggests, is 'deeply political' (2007, 5). Only perhaps by identifying and theorizing power plays through analysing the geography of care, might we move towards reconstructing some of these institutions and structures.

Thinking about Lawson's (2007) invitation to consider care in other contexts and fields, this paper suggests that care is a crucial part of human mobility as it relates to migration and asylum systems. It is particularly relevant to much of the practices and policies being applied and enacted in the blurred space of the Mediterranean Sea. Care intersects with migration in this space in three ways: first it is bound up in an ethical or moral obligation to help those in need; second there is a legal responsibility to care for those found struggling in the Mediterranean, and third, there is a responsibility under international law for European Union States to protect and care for migrants or refugees intercepted at its borders. These intersections although not interchangeable are sometimes difficult to disentangle.

Some of those making the treacherous journey across the Mediterranean during the height of the migration 'crisis' were seeking asylum or had been displaced by conflict. Refugee status is a social category, a part of which expectation of care is assumed. Under the definition of refugees as set out by the 1951 United Nations Refugee Convention, a person assigned the label of refugee should be able to avail of specific forms of care and protection. Under its terms a refugee is a person 'who owing to a well-founded fear of being persecuted for reasons of race, religion, nationality, membership of a particular social group or political opinion, is outside the country of his nationality and is unable or, owing to such fear, is unwilling to avail himself of the protection of that country; or who, not having a nationality and being outside the country of his former habitual residence as a result of such events, is unable or, owing to such fear, is unwilling to return to it' (UN 1951). Historically, States have held the principle role in assigning refugee status but since 2013 the United Nations Refugee Agency (UNRA) has become increasingly involved if European States are unwilling or cannot engage in this process. As Zetter (2014) suggests governments in Europe use a variety of extra territorial mechanisms to ensure that migrants do not achieve that status within their borders. Mountz's (2011) research into the offshoring practices of interdiction highlights how migrants are deliberately stopped from researching Europe's shores in order to ensure that they do not have the right to apply for asylum. Much of this practice has been led by Frontex, the pan-European agency tasked with policing external borders. Frontex, as Mainwaring and Brigden (2016, 15) observe largely 'depicts migrant journeys as unidimensional and unidirectional lines towards the EU'. They are 'decontextualized and depoliticized' which have an almost dehumanizing effect. In response to the volume of migrants and asylum seekers crossing the Mediterranean in 2015, it was reframed as the European Border and Coastguard Agency. It plays, as Williams and Mountz (2016) note, a critical role in the militarization of the Mediterranean and is explicitly involved in practices that ensure that vessels carrying migrants will not reach Europe's shores.

In Article 33, paragraph 1 of the Refugee Convention outlines or defines the principle of *non-refoulement*. According to this statute, refugees cannot be returned to their countries of origin for fear of persecution. This effectively implies that more layers of care may be needed for those refugees who cannot be returned, subjecting States to varying economic, social and political ramifications. Zetter (2016) further argues that some EU states deliberately complicate the process of labelling and this has important implications for their duty of care towards those who seek refuge. Echoing this sentiment, Andersson's (2014) research documents lengthy stays for those seeking care at border checkpoints across Europe. He argues that temporality is used as a weapon or tactic with serious economic implications. Participants in his study liken their protracted periods of detention (while waiting to be processed and labelled) to being imprisoned in places of incarceration that are notorious with human right violations or abuses. In these in-between spaces, as a form of biopolitical control of the subjects within them, care is rationed, and individuals are marginalized. 'Crossing borders and transgressing the maintenance of boundaries, refugees bring into view the contested and contingent nature of national limits and identities. Asylum seekers are literally matter out of place' (Andersson 2014, 796). Those seeking asylum or refugee status are kept in extra-territorial spaces outside the margins of the everyday.

Evaluating a Duty of Care within Legislative Frameworks

Before thinking about how actors across different scales conceptualize care it is important primarily to review the legal frameworks that influence the ways in which irregular migrants experience care. I draw on Fischer-Lescano's et al. (2009) important work to sketch out the legal texts that shape the behaviours of macro and micro level actors which find themselves in high-pressure environments dealing with sea-borne migrants. Article 98 of the United Nations Convention on the Law at Sea establishes the legal duties of vessels that are confronted with lives at risk at sea. It states that:

> Every State shall require the master of a ship flying its flag, in so far as he can do so without serious danger to the ship, the crew or the passengers, to render assistance to any person found at sea in danger of being lost, [and] to proceed with all possible speed to the rescue of persons in distress, if informed of their need of assistance, in so far as such action may reasonably be expected of him.

This principle sets a precedent for both European States and vessels. By linking the 'identity' of the ship with the sovereignty or identity of a specific State, the duty of care is expanded beyond the individual sailing a particular vessel. The Article continues to extend the responsibility of care to coastal States arguing that every 'coastal State shall promote the establishment, operation and maintenance of an adequate and effective SAR service regarding safety on and over the sea and, where circumstances so require, by way of mutual regional arrangements cooperate with neighbouring States for this purpose' (1951). This particularly broad remit tasks neighbouring states with carrying additional responsibility for those in danger. Yet it does not offer any clarity on the nature of 'mutual regional arrangements' and leaves considerable scope for contestation and resistance between and across EU States who are at odds about their respective duty of care.

While Article 98 sets out the legal duty of care towards those found at sea, a second legal framework that is increasingly used to navigate modes of responsibility is Article 2, paragraph 1 on the 1982 Law of the Sea which delineates the territorial jurisdiction of States. It suggests that the territory (and thus the responsibility) of the State extends to 12 nautical miles out to sea. If migrants are picked up within 12 nautical miles of a State's shore, then it is their responsibility to initiate the caretaking and caregiving process. This legislation, couched within the geopolitics of Europe, is increasingly having implications for whether neighbouring vessels will 'obey' it. Williams and Mountz (2016) suggests that the securitization of migration in Europe, framed within narratives of othering, criminality and even terrorism, intersects with these decisions. 'By scripting migrants and would-be asylum seekers as criminal and security threats the rationale is set forth discursively for their distancing through exclusionary measures or bureaucratic management off-shore' (Williams and Mountz 2016, 32).

The controversial Dublin System which deals with asylum is also problematic. The system works on the premise that requests for asylum are dealt with primarily by the principle State of entry. This has however meant that the challenge of processing and dealing with requests from seaborne migrants who want to seek asylum lie principally with a small number of southern States such as Spain, Malta, Greece and Italy (see Kasparek 2016). Decisions about the status of 'Dublined' individuals who wish to travel through Europe to meet family and friends often fall to the States at their original point of entry, although the unification of families is on paper supposed to be a key criterion in assigning care. The geopolitical wrangling over the responsibility of care under Dublin in relation to migration across Europe has occasioned a fractious debate that sheds some light on the 'gulf that seems to have opened up between the way in which policy makers conceptualize forced migration and the way in which it is conceptualized by advocates and activists' (Turton 2003 cited in

Mouzourakis 2014). These complex and contradictory modes of responsibility across multiple scales have profound implications for the geography of care in Europe.

Problems invariably arise for those in need of immediate or critical care whenever Article 2 collides with Article 98. As they do whenever there is no time or space to work through nautical miles, legal frameworks or systems of governance. How should 'boat people' (Pugh 2004) act when they encounter individuals whose lives are at immediate risk? How does care play out in these emotive and challenging spaces within a context of fraught geopolitical relationships? The scale of irregular migration to Europe across the Mediterranean means that humanitarian organizations, SAR vessels, individual states, supranational organizations and the multiple publics face debates around responsibility and care in challenging environments that blurs ethical/moral, territorial, legislative and geopolitical boundaries. This is further complicated by a contested discourse where the social categories of refugees and migrants often come into conflict with legal categories. The Aquarius case offers an intriguing window into this complex arena of blurred borders and conflicting modes of responsibility.

Humanitarian Vessels in the Mediterranean: humanizing Migrants?

Humanitarian work is grounded in the principles of 'humanity, impartiality and neutrality', attempting to occupy a 'symbolic space, separate from politics' (Cusumano 2018, 389). Those who undertake this type of vocational work do so because they want to occupy a caring space that delivers immediate and critical care to those who are in need. Bretherton (2006) suggests 'liberal unitarians and deontologists argue that liberal democracies in principle, owe a duty of care to all humanity and by implication that borders should be in principle, open'. This 'liberal will-to-care' observed by Reid-Henry (2013) and imagined through humanitarian organizations has grown steadily since the end of the Cold War, as have care-based interventions by specific States. Yet the latter has often resulted in conflicting geopolitical imaginaries and tensions (Reid-Henry 2013).

Rozakou (2017) charts the critical role that NGOs and small charities have played in alleviating the suffering occasioned by large-scale migration. This work has, however, has become much more difficult given the growing politicization and militarization of aid (Cusumano 2017). It is becoming intrinsically difficult for the humanitarian sector to remain 'aloof from Western governments' agendas (2017, 92). It is hardly surprisingly then, that humanitarian organizations have increasingly found themselves working at a very complex set of spatial and legal scales that often collide with governance, legislation, political systems and public opinion.

As humanitarian space 'on dry land' shrinks (Cusumano 2018, 388), efforts to engage in SAR at sea have increased (Stierl 2016). Cuttitta (2018) posits that such organizations are playing a growing and much contested role in managing borders. They have since 2015 been working alongside the coastal SAR teams of southern States, such as Italy and Malta. This relationship has been and continues to be fraught with controversy (see Williams 2015). On the one hand, NGOs are assisting and helping coordinate many of the operations. They have played a vital role in rescuing migrants and refugees in the absence of established maritime agencies. On the other, charities and NGOs have found themselves working unilaterally without the consent of States and alongside traffickers and smugglers. Tazzioli's (2016) research into humanitarian visibility in the Mediterranean highlights the growing complexities that NGOs face in attempting to administer care. Visibility, she argues, is one of the pillars of intervention. Since 2015, NGOs and charities have worked tirelessly to increase their own visibility to migrants and to detect ships in trouble. They have developed 'regimes of visibility', defining what must be seen and what can go unnoticed or undetected. By 2016 their willingness to be seen as the 'good border spectacle' had in many ways transformed their capacity to detect into their almost inescapable duty to rescue' (Tazzioli 2016, 577).

Humanitarian involvement in SAR activities in the Mediterranean came sharply into focus in June 2018 when the fate of the Aquarius captured the world's attention. Carrying some 600 of migrants, it became stranded off the coast of Italy. Operating under the humanitarian organization, Medicine Sans Borders (henceforth MSF) at Sea, the vessel attempted to work alongside SAR organizations to help save lives on a particularly treacherous route between Libya and Europe. MSF have been involved in SAR efforts in the Mediterranean since early 2016. It has a large membership and relies heavily on sponsorship and public support. Social media technologies have been critically important in helping MSF and other NGOs engage in the process of humanizing refugees and defending their duty of care. The galvanization of humanitarian intervention not just in the Mediterranean but across the globe has been enabled by the explosion of digital technologies which are enabling like-minded individuals to come together to collectively initiate action to help those in need. For Reid-Henry (2013, 41) contemporary humanitarian work 'allows Western citizens to better understand how their wealth and privilege intersects with poverty and suffering elsewhere'.

MSF works closely with the Maritime Rescue Centre in Rome and abides by maritime legislation. They patrol in international waters during the day and only move closer to state borders if lives are seriously at risk. MSF assert that as a humanitarian agency involved in SAR, it does not have a mandate or means to label or assess the immigration status of the people it assists. It 'provides medical care without judgment and strongly believes that no human being should drown when the means exist to prevent it'. It persistently has lobbied for 'a Europe that protects human lives' (MSF 2018). This stance of not engaging in a labelling strategy when individuals need critical care is shared by other NGOs operating in the Mediterranean. Proactiva Open Arms is a Spanish NGO vessel which uses similar powerful images and language to portray its objectives in its campaigns. With the strapline 'Either a life is saved, or a death is silenced, it has been involved in multiple rescue operations. Visitors to its website or Twitter feed are confronted with emotive images of individuals that it has rescued. One image shows a child in trouble in the sea with the question. 'Should I tell him there's already poor people in my country? Or should I save his life? (Open Arms, 2018). These images and words present a simple choice between life and death-a choice that does not include immigration quotas, assigning status or determining nautical miles.

NGOs in the Mediterranean have also suggested that the subsequent refusal of Aquarius, first by Italy, then Malta contravened not only maritime legislation but also were a contradiction of European values (see Jones 2018). The troubles faced by Aquarius were to become a constant feature of 2018. Following the first crisis Aquarius was stripped of its state registration and ordered to suspend operations. After a brief interim period, it found itself at the centre of yet another geopolitical controversy when a new crisis emerged a few months later. It intercepted 141 migrants in distress in the Mediterranean and attempted to dock in Italy. However, Italy demanded that Britain take responsibility for the migrants as the ship was registered to Gibraltar, a British overseas territory. It also suggested that foul play was involved suggesting that the ship was also registered as a survey vessel, as opposed to a humanitarian vessel. Malta responded that it would not accept the vessel and would in fact strip the ship of its registration status. The vessel was stranded in international waters between Italy and Malta waiting for a State to open its borders. Weeks later, a Tunisian vessel, the Sarost 5 suffered a similar fate and was stranded at sea for over three weeks.

NGO activity in the Mediterranean has pulled European States into debates about care, morality and values. As Reid-Henry (2013) observes humanitarianism has 'set limits on state power in terms of what we might today call 'human' rights, but only to the extent that it also made possible a mobius-like recuperation of sovereignty, the power over life, in other ways' (Reid-Henry 2013, 425). States have in retaliation increasingly criticized NGOs for facilitating something much more sinister in Europe that jeopardizes not just the social and economic equilibrium but also the security of national borders. Humanitarian organizations in the Mediterranean have found themselves operating uncomfortably alongside not only military and law enforcement stakeholders but smugglers and traffickers (Cusumano 2018), further complicating their duty of care. They have been accused of breaching human rights in facilitating illegal activities that contravene human rights. Writing in a different context about the tensions between humanitarianism: 'For many people, it is almost counter-intuitive to have to consider that humanitarian action may also have a dark side which compromises as well as helps the people whose suffering it seeks to assuage' (Sims, 1997, 244). Kennedy's (2005, 6) research into the darker sides of humanitarianism suggests that organizations need to take more responsibility and reflect on the inherent power they hold and how that impacts the lives of other ' there is scarcely a humanitarian practice that does not act as if governance were elsewhere – in government, statecraft, the member states, the states' parties, the Security Council, the field, the headquarters, the empire. And yet we do rule. We exercise power and affect distributions among people. Let us no longer avert our eyes from humanitarian rulership'.

The Role of European States: geopoliticizing Care

Pugh (2000) suggests that the prominence of the neo-liberal agenda across Europe with its goals of achieving successful economic integration has been accompanied by the tightening of immigration controls at the level of the State. Increased anxiety over the so-called refugee crisis amongst European States is perhaps symptomatic of a much deeper renegotiation of the meaning and form of the nation-state (Mitzen 2018). Wealthy States, as Reid-Henry (2013) notes, manage that wealth through immigration controls and engage in dichotomous acts of care and control. Restricting mobility however is a complex and contradictory process. 'A limited opening up of the state to those in need', as Reid-Henry observes, 'has as its counterpart thereduction of identities to rather limiting form of biological citizenship Petryna (2003, 31) notes that 'a limited opening up of the State to those in need thus has as its counterpart the reduction of identities to rather limiting forms of 'biological citizenship'. Across the European Union the free movement of individuals coexists with a hardening of immigration policy towards non-EU citizens.

The response to sea-borne migrants in the Mediterranean in the summer of 2018 was mixed. The new Italian populist right-wing government sought to reframe its duty of care. Following the docking of Aquarius in Spain, the Interior Minister Matteo Salvini suggested that the Italian government had scored its first victory in government claiming, 'We have opened a front in Brussels' (Kirchgaessner, Tondo, and Jones 2018). Opening the channels of communication with the European Union was critically important for Salvini who became interior minister only weeks before the Aquarius was refused entry. 'We are contacting the European commission so that it can fulfil its duties towards Italy that have never been respected' (Kirchgaessner, Tondo, and Jones 2018). Salvini was referring to the disproportionate volume of migrants and refugees reaching Europe through Italy (BBC News 2018b), an issue not resolved through the EU-Turkish pact in late 2017. This pact was designed to curb the number of migrants arriving in Europe. Under its terms, migrants would be held and processed in Turkey, devolving responsibility from European States. Significantly, UNHRC data suggests that the volume of sea arrivals to Italy has in fact decreased dramatically. In 2014, 170,110 migrants arrived by sea. This decreased to 23,370 by 2018 with numbers down to just over 10 k by November 2019 (UNHCR 2019). A few days later, the Italian government once again refused a US warship assisting a German SAR vessel (Sea Watch) entry. It was carrying 41 migrants and 12 dead bodies it had intercepted off the coast of Libya. Significantly and paradoxically, an Italian coastguard vessel carrying 932 refugees and two dead bodies was granted permission by Rome shortly after these refusals to dock at the Sicilian port of Catania. Sea-Watch (Cockburn 2018), infuriated by the Italian stance said the decision to allow some vessels over others highlighted the 'double standards' of the Italian government. The United Nations Refugee Agency weighed in stating, 'It is wrong, dangerous and immoral to keep rescue ships wandering the Mediterranean while governments compete on who can take the least responsibility.' Salvini said in an interview with the *Corriere della Sera* newspaper in June, 'Ships belonging to foreign organizations and flying foreign flags cannot dictate Italy's immigration policy .... we will not change (our position) on ships belonging to non-governmental organizations. Saving lives is a duty. Turning Italy into a refugee camp is not' (DW.Com 2018). Salvini's stance and discourse can be read as an attempt to reframe the humanitarian component of the duty of care by conflating it with state-based arguments about borders and territory. A key part of its rhetoric plays on a heightened sense of nationalism whereby Italy's policy on immigration will not be dictated by external stakeholders such as humanitarian vessels, nor by European neighbours.

Italy's refusal to engage with NGO vessels triggered something of a geopolitical standoff as European States sought to position themselves ethically and politically. Malta too, refused the Aquarius entry, stating that as a sovereign country no other State should dictate its policies on immigration. It stated that it did not have the capacity to care for over 600 migrants nor was it 'appropriate' to do so (Denti 2018). French President, Emanuel Macron attacked Italy for being 'irresponsible' suggesting its actions contravened maritime law. He later however changed his tone adding his voice to critics who framed NGO vessels as helping violent gangs trafficking people to Europe (Euroactiv.com, 2018). Commenting on yet another rescue operation by a Norwegian vessel in September, he suggested that it had broken 'all the rules when it took migrants onto its boat'. He added 'We cannot permanently accept this situation. In the end we are playing into the hands of smugglers by reducing the risks of the journey'.

Fischer-Lescano, Löhr, and Tohidipur (2009), note that governments 'occasionally argue that State border controls, particularly on the high seas, take place in a space where refugee and human rights law do not apply'. In this blurred thirdspace where responsibilities are unclear, the process of dehumanization is at its most visible. It is important to note that the care of migrants is a process, not one singular act. When sea-borne migrants are rescued through an act of care it triggers a response that does not necessarily end when that refugee disembarks from a vessel. Some journalists pointed out that the controversy surrounding Aquarius simply illustrates the problem with the Dublin system that they suggested it appeared to be breaking with the pressure of the migration challenge. The geopolitical wrangling between States has sometimes sought to evade the scales of care and responsibility, serving to dehumanize individuals. As Taylor (2018, 8) observes, the dehumanization of migrants is increasing throughout Europe. Writing in the aftermath on an EU summit in June 2018 to curb immigration, he continues: 'the cries of those downing in the Mediterranean were drowned out … .by the sound of the Continent's leaders washing their hands of the misfortune of asylum seekers to save their political skins.'

Public Discourse: Contributing to the Debate

It is important to note that the decisions of politicians and the actions of NGOs do not exist in a vacuum. Their actions are shaped by and in turn shape and inform their respective publics. Pugh, writing in 2001, suggested that the hegemonic discourse in the West centred on the idea that migrants and refugees arriving by boat to Europe through the Mediterranean were a threat and that their presence would have profound social and political implications for European States. Sea-borne migrants were traditionally viewed as a welfare issue. That discourse has changed significantly in tone since 2013 (see Dempsey and McDowell 2018) with migration increasingly being framed by parts of the media as both a threat to security and its impact likened to that of a natural disaster, an unstoppable, devastating force. The role of humanitarian organizations operating in the Mediterranean reveals the fragmented contours of public discourse. The emergence of an 'anxious politics' (Modest and Koning cited in Dempsey and McDowell 2018) has given rise to an increase in support for populist ideologies. An analysis of tweets and comments posted on the social media accounts of @MSF during the Aquarius controversy revealed a particularly potent strand of public backlash, likening the organization's activities to that of people smugglers. As one twitter user warned, 'Water taxi … take the *****s back. Illegal migrants funded by Soros &MSF'. Another wrote, 'Disgusting. Economic migrants can apply legally'. While yet another responded, 'You're not humanitarian, you're smugglers'. Tweet upon tweet accused the organization of people smuggling 'You are one of the biggest smugglers in the Med. You should all be arrested and imprisoned'. The tone of these specific comments reveals something of the volatility of care geographies in relation to migration.

Another recurrent theme in the online exchange of comments served to denigrate the status of those rescued at sea. One prominent thread involved a story of some twenty missing migrants who disembarked Aquarius in Valencia. As one user noted '23 of the migrants who arrived in Spain have already disappeared. Who could have seen this coming?' The fate of Aquarius received much attention across the European press. The UK's BBC led with the headline 'The Aquarius: Migrant taxi-service or charitable rescue? while *The Independent* newspaper's editorial led with an opinion piece entitled 'Why Italy was right to not let migrant boat dock' (Cockburn 2018). Editorials in Spain suggested that each of the migrants who arrived in Spain would receive 'resonalized attention' (The Local 2018). An analysis of some online commentary paints a very different picture of the activities of humanitarian organizations stripping out morality and care ethics. They present such organizations as actors who deliberately intervene in a crisis to prop up or expedite the smuggling process.

This strand of resistance has not been confined to embittered online exchanges. Defend Europe, far-right organization with an anti-Islam and anti-immigration ethos, funded a vessel to transverse the Mediterranean in an effort to stop trafficking and send migrants and would-be asylum seekers 'back to Africa' (Bulman 2017). It aimed to curb the work of humanitarian SAR activities.

Conclusion

Ambrosi (Embling 2018) suggests that the issue of SAR in the Mediterranean is very much a grey zone that blurs boundaries and speaks to deep-rooted anxieties about geopolitical imaginings of Europe. This paper exposes some of those grey zones and presents an insight into the ways in which care geographies intersect with governance, ethics and geopolitics within the context of migration. In applying theories of care to a reading of European migration, it urges for a more nuanced appraisal of how the making and unmaking of refugees collide with fiercely contested notions of how we should, or are willing to, care for those in need. In charting the battles between various actors and stakeholders, the paper contributes to the growing sense that migrants have become pawns in wider geopolitical battles over E.U polices on inclusion and exclusion. The controversy over humanitarian vessels in the Mediterranean underlines the inherent complexity of legislative frameworks that perhaps are not fit for purpose as migration evolves. It also raises serious questions for trying to administer care in a vacuum where the ethical and moral impulse to save lives, overlaps with the politics of migration on multiple scales.

Popke (2006) suggests that we need to continue to develop ways of thinking through our responsibilities towards unseen others, and to cultivate a renewed sense of social interconnectedness. But where does care begin and end and how do we navigate blurred territorial and moral boundaries? These are important questions, not just for E.U policymakers but for humanitarian organizations and NGOs that operate in challenging conditions. Sea-borne migrants pose a specific set of complex challenges. There is perhaps merit in the idea that the very legislation that is intended to assign labels that should in theory provide migrants and refugees with care, often serves to render them 'less than human' (DeBono 2013, 60), and results in States attempting to circumvent their duty of care. The geopoliticizing of care reveals a Europe with very different ideas about borders, rights and responsibilities.

In December 2018, MSF announced that it was suspending all SAR operations in the Mediterranean following 'sustained attacks by European States'. The organization had grown tired of the incessant geopolitical wrangling. Italy's Interior Minister tweeted in response 'Fewer sailings, fewer landings, fewer deaths. That's good' (BBC News 2018b). This fractious online exchange between two key actors underscores the difficulties discussed in this paper, in navigating care across blurred boundaries and at different scales. Cusumano (2018) warns that SAR operations and interventions in the Mediterranean undertaken by humanitarian organizations is simply getting too difficult and is perhaps 'incompatible with strict interpretation of principles of independence, neutral and impartiality'. At stake however, are the lives of individuals who make the decision to cross a treacherous stretch of water in hope of a better life.

Acknowledgments

I'd like to thank Kara Dempsey and Orhon Myadar for their editorial advice and direction on this Special Edition. I'd also like to thank the three anonymous reviewers for their constructive comments and suggestions.

References

Andersson, R. 2014. Time and the migrant other: European border controls and the temporal economics of illegality. *American Anthropologist* 116 (4):795–809. doi:10.1111/aman.12148.
BBC News. 2018a. The Aquarius: Migrant taxi service or charitable rescuers? June 20. Accessed June 09, 2019. https://www.bbc.co.uk/news/world-europe-44581764
BBC News. 2018b. MSF ship Aquarius ends migrant rescue in the Mediterranean December 7. Accessed February 10, 2019. https://www.bbc.co.uk/news/world-europe-46477158
Bleiker, R., D. Campbell., E. Hutchison, and X. Nicholson. 2013. The visual dehumanisation of refugees. *Australian Journal of Political Science* 48 (4):398–416. doi:10.1080/10361146.2013.840769.
Bretherton, L. 2006. The duty of care to refugees: Christian cosmopolitanism and the hallowing of bare life. *Studies in Christian Ethics* 19 (1):39–61. doi:10.1177/0953946806062268.
Bulman, M. 2017. Far right organisation sends boats to confront organisations rescuing refugees to take them back to Africa, *The Independent* July 17. Accessed January 10, 2019.

https://www.independent.co.uk/news/world/europe/anti-immigrant-ship-mediterranean-ngo-ships-refugee-crisis-migrant-boats-people-smugglers-defend-a7838731.html

Carvalho, A. 2008. Media (ted) discourse and society: Rethinking the framework of critical discourse analysis. *Journalism Studies* 9 (2):161–77. doi:10.1080/14616700701848162.

Cockburn, H. 2018. Italian foreign ministry summons French ambassador as tensions mount over port closures to refugee rescue boats. *The Independent* June 13. Accessed January 12, 2019. https://www.independent.co.uk/news/world/europe/italy-port-closures-refugees-mediterranean-matteo-salvini-aquarius-emmanuel-macron-a8396916.html

Conradson, D. 2003. Geographies of care: Spaces, practices and experiences. *Social and Cultural Geography* 4 (1):451–54. doi:10.1080/1464936032000137894.

Cusumano, E. 2017. Emptying the sea with a spoon? Non-governmental providers of migrant search and rescue in the Mediterranean. *Marine Policy* 75:91–98. doi:10.1016/j.marpol.2016.10.008.

Cusumano, E. 2018. The sea as humanitarian space: Non-governmental search and rescue dilemmas on the Central Mediterranean migratory route. *Mediterranean Politics* 23 (3):387–94. doi:10.1080/13629395.2017.1302223.

Cuttitta, P. 2018. Repoliticization through search and rescue? Humanitarian NGOs and migration management in the central mediterranean. *Geopolitics* 23 (3):632–60. doi:10.1080/14650045.2017.1344834.

Davidson, J., and C. Milligan. 2004. Embodying emotion sensing space: introducing emotional geographies. *Social and Cultural Geography* 5 (1):523–32. doi:10.1080/1464936042000317677.

DeBono, D. 2013. 'Less than human': The detention of irregular immigrants in Malta. *Race and Class* 55 (2):60–81. doi:10.1177/0306396813497880.

Dempsey, K. E., and S. McDowell. 2018. Disaster depictions and geopolitical representations in Europe's migration 'Crisis'. *Geoforum* 98.153–60.

Denti, A. 2018. Migrant rescue returned to sea. *Reuters*, August 1. Accessed February 20, 2019. https://uk.reuters.com/article/uk-europe-migrants-ngo/migrant-rescue-ship-aquarius-returns-to-sea-after-italy-malta-dispute-idUKKBN1KM50U

DW.Com. (2018) Italy stands by decision to reject boat of migrants as row with France escalates. June 13. Accessed September 12, 2018. https://www.dw.com/en/italy-stands-by-decision-to-reject-boat-of-migrants-as-row-with-france-escalates/a-44199388

Embling, D. 2018. Aquarius: the symptom of a bigger disease? Euronews.com June 14, Available at https://www.euronews.com/2018/06/14/aquarius-the-symptom-ofa-bigger-dis ease -Accessed 10 December 2019

Euoractiv. 2018. France adds its voice to stop NGO ships from acting as 'taxis'. June 28. Accessed February 20, 2019. https://www.euractiv.com/section/future-eu/news/france-adds-its-voice-to-stop-ngo-ships-from-acting-as-taxis/

Fischer-Lescano, A., T. Löhr, and T. Tohidipur. 2009. Border controls at sea: Requirements under international human rights and refugee law. *International Journal of Refugee Law* 21 (2):256–96. doi:10.1093/ijrl/eep008.

Fisher, B., and J. Tronto. 1990. Toward a feminist theory of caring. *Circles of care: Work and identity in women's lives* 35–62.

Held, V. 2006. *The ethics of care: personal, political and global*. Oxford, UK: Oxford University Press.

Hughes, B., L. McKie, D. Hopkins, and N. Watson. 2005. Love's labours lost? Feminism, the Disabled People's Movement and an ethic of care. *Sociology* 39:259–75. doi:10.1177/0038038505050538.

Hyndman, J. 2000. Managing displacement: Refugees and the politics of humanitarianism. University of Minnesota Press:Minneapolis.

Hyndman, J., and A. Mountz. 2008. Another brick in the wall? Neo-refoulement and the externalization of asylum by Australia and Europe. *Government and Opposition* 43 (2):249–69. doi:10.1111/j.1477-7053.2007.00251.x.

Jennifer Mitzen (2018) Anxious community: EU as (in)security community, European Security, 27:3, 393-413, DOI: 10.1080/09662839.2018.1497985.

Jones, S. (2018) Aquarius refusal was a betrayal of European values, says charity boss. *The Guardian*, June 17. Accessed March 30, 2019. https://www.theguardian.com/world/2018/jun/17/aquarius-refusal-was-betrayal-of-european-values-says-charity-boss

Kasparek, B. 2016. Complementing schengen: The Dublin system and the European border and migration regime. In *Migration policy and practice. migration, diasporas and citizenship*, ed. H. Bauder and C. Matheis. New York: Palgrave Macmillan. 59-78.

Kennedy, D. 2005. *The dark sides of virtue: Reassessing international humanitarianism*. Princeton, New Jersey: Princeton University Press.

Kirchgaessner, S., L. Tondo, and S. Jones. 2018. Italian minister declares victory as Spain accepts rescue boat. *The Guardian*, August 11. Accessed August 30, 2018. https://www.theguardian.com/world/2018/jun/11/un-calls-for-migrant-ship-to-be-allowed-to-dock-in-italian-port

Lawson, V. 2007. Geographies of care and responsibility. *Annals of the Association of American Geographers* 97 (1):1–11. doi:10.1111/j.1467-8306.2007.00520.x.

Mainwaring, C. 2016. Migrant agency: Negotiating borders and migration controls. *Migration Studies* 4 (3):289–308. doi:10.1093/migration/mnw013.

Mainwaring, C., and N. Brigden. 2016. Beyond the border: clandestine migration journeys. *Geopolitics* 21 (2):243–62. doi:10.1080/14650045.2016.1165575.

McDowell, S., M. Braniff., and J. Murphy. 2017. Zero-sum politics in contested spaces: The unintended consequences of legislative peacebuilding in Northern Ireland. *Political Geography* 61:193–202. doi:10.1016/j.polgeo.2017.09.001.

McKie, L., S. Gregory, and S. Bowlby. 2002. Shadow times: The temporal and spatial frameworks and experiences of caring and working. *Sociology* 36 (4):897–924. doi:10.1177/003803850203600406.

Milligan, C., and J. Wiles. 2010. Landscapes of care. *Progress in Human Geography* 34 (6):736–54. doi:10.1177/0309132510364556.

Mountz, A. 2011. Where asylum-seekers wait: Feminist counter-topographies of sites between states. *Gender, Place and Culture* 18 (3):381–99. doi:10.1080/0966369X.2011.566370.

Mouzourakis, M. 2014. 'We need to talk about Dublin'. Responsibility under the Dublin system as a blockage to asylum–burden sharing in the European Union. *Refugee Studies Centre Working Paper Series* No. 105.

MSF. (2018) Mediterranean Search and Rescue. https://www.msf.org.uk/country/mediterranean-search-and-rescue

Open Arms (2018) @openarms_found/Twitterhttps://twitter.com/openarms_found.ref_src=twsrc%5Egoogle%7Ctwcamp%5Eserp%7Ctwgr%5Eautho. Accessed November 29, 2018.

Petyrna, A. 2003.Life exposed: biological citizens after Chernobyl. Princeton University Press, New Jersey

Popke, J. 2006. Geography and Ethics: Everyday mediations through care and consumption. *Progress in Human Geography* 30 (4):504–12. doi:10.1191/0309132506ph622pr.

Pugh, M. 2000. *Europe's boat people: Maritime cooperation in the Mediterranean*. Institute for Security Studies, Paris: Western European Union.

Pugh, M. 2004. Drowning not waving: Boat people and humanitarianism at sea. *Journal of Refugee Studies* 17 (1):50–69. doi:10.1093/jrs/17.1.50.

Reid-Henry, S. M. 2013. Humanitarianism as liberal diagnostic: Humanitarian reason and the political rationalities of the liberal will-to-care. *Transactions of British Geographers* 39:418–31. doi:10.1111/tran.12029.

Rozakou, K. 2017. Solidarity #humanitarianism: The blurred boundaries of humanitarianism in Greece. *Etnofoor* 29 (2):99–104.

Slim, H. 1997. Doing the right thing: relief agencies, moral dilemmas and moral responsibility in political emergencies and war. *Disasters* 21 (3):244–57. doi:10.1111/1467-7717.00059.

Stierl, M. 2016. A sea of struggle – Activist border interventions in the Mediterranean Sea. *Citizenship Studies* 20 (5):561–78. doi:10.1080/13621025.2016.1182683.

Taylor, P. 2018. EU leaders to migrants: Go home and stay home. *Politico EU*, July 03 https://www.politico.eu/article/europe-migration-refugees-drop-dead-angela-merkel-matteo-salvini-libya-italy-germany-refugee/ Accessed 10 October 2018.

Tazzioli, M. 2016. Eurosur, humanitarian visibility, and (nearly) real-time mapping in the Mediterranean. *ACME* 15 (3):561.

The Local Spain. (2018) What next for the Aquarius in Spain? June 14. Accessed September 07, 2018. https://www.thelocal.es/20180614/what-next-for-aquarius-migrants-in-spain

Turton, D. 2003. Conceptualising Forced Migration, RSC Working Paper No. 12. https://www.rsc.ox.ac.uk/files/files-1/wp12-conceptualising-forced-migration-2003.pdf Accessed 12 June 2019.

UNHCR-The 1951 Convention Available at https://www.unhcr.org/uk/1951-refugee-convention.html. Accessed 02 June 2019.

UNHCR. (2019) Operational portal sea operations: Italy. Accessed 20 November 2019. https://data2.unhcr.org/en/situations/mediterranean/location/5205

UNOCHRA. (2018) UNHCR welcomes Aquarius resolution, but stresses need for more predictable approach to disembarkation. August 15. Accessed February 10, 2019. https://www.unhcr.org/news/press/2018/8/5b73d04f4/unhcr-welcomes-aquarius-resolution-stresses-need-predictable-approach-disembarkation.html

Williams, J. M. 2015. From humanitarian exceptionalism to contingent care: Care and enforcement at the humanitarian border. *Political Geography* 47:11–20. doi:10.1016/j.polgeo.2015.01.001.

Williams, K., and A. Mountz. 2016. Rising tide–analysing the relationship between externalization and migrant deaths and boat losses. In *Externalizing migration management: Europe, North America and the Spread of 'remote control 'practices*, ed. R. Zaiotti, 31–49. New York: Routledge.

Wintour, P., L. Tondo, and S. Kirchgaessar (2018) Southern mayors defy Italian coalition to offer safe port to rescue vessel but may need coastguard cooperation. *The Guardian*, June 11. Accessed September 21, 2018. https://www.theguardian.com/world/2018/jun/10/italy-shuts-ports-to-rescue-boat-with-629-migrants-on-board

Zetter, R. 2014. The problem of externalising Europe's borders. InShifting

Place, Displacement and Belonging: The Story of Abdi

Orhon Myadar

ABSTRACT
In traditional geopolitical discourses, an individual's very being is routinely tied to and predicated upon the sanctity of the individual's nation-state. The global refugee regime operates upon this assumption and regulates those who have been forcibly displaced from their homelands. Feminist geopolitics offers a way to see beyond the rigid boundaries of nation-states and attend to the embodied, lived, intimate and everyday experiences of people and their situated realities in any given time/space intersection. In this article, I explore questions of place and displacement through the story of one man's journey from his village in Somalia to his eventual resettlement in Tucson, Arizona. Through Abdi's story, this article seeks to contribute to geographic understanding of the immanence of place to self as it relates to displacement and forced mobility. Abdi's story and his journey from Migwa to Tucson illustrate the nomad potential of his connection and disconnection to various places he has inhabited. His story and lived experience provide a nuanced example of the context of human relations with the places they inhabit and how these relations are much more fluid and porous than that assumed in the model of the 'geographical self'- the self that is deeply rooted in and defined by places. This story-based approach reclaims human agency in the dyadic connection between place and self and centers individual experience in a geographic study of forced mobility and displacement.

Stories matter. Many stories matter. Stories have been used to dispossess and to malign, but stories can also be used to empower and to humanize. Stories can break the dignity of a people, but stories can also repair that broken dignity.

Chimamanda Ngozi Adichie (2009)

Introduction

I first met Abdi[1] when he took my political geography class in 2014. As a part of the class discussion on forced mobility and displacement, he offered to share his story of leaving his home country and growing up in a refugee camp in Kenya. In his talk, Abdi shared his fraught connections with Somalia, the country of his birth, and what it was like for him to be the Other in his homeland. He also talked about his life in a refugee camp where he spent 13 years and his continued negotiation of his sense of belonging in Tucson, where he finally feels at home. He told his story with so much humility, passion and thoughtfulness that his classmates later on shared that it was one of the most inspiring, humbling and touching stories they had ever heard.

Today more than 68.5 million people are forcibly displaced worldwide, over half of them children- the highest number on record since the UN's Refugee Agency started collecting statistics (UNHCR 2018). Despite the grim number, it is easy to turn one's attention away from this disembodied, giant statistic. But when hearing someone, in flesh and blood, talk about his own individual story and lived struggles, it is not easy to ignore or look away. That was the case when Abdi shared his story with the class and when he provided additional details later on in a recorded interview as a part of my project on the voices of Tucson's refugee communities.

In understanding Abdi's story, I turn to the Nigerian novelist Chimamanda Ngozi Adichie's1977 inspirational talk on the "danger of a single story" (2009). In her talk, Adichie discusses a principle of *nkali* in storytelling. According to Adichie, *nkali* is an Igbo word which roughly means "to be greater than another". As Adichie suggests, the principle of nkali shapes stories in the ways "how they are told, who tells them, when they're told, how many stories are told." By centring this article on Abdi's story, the article thus aims to reorient the nkali from a typical refugee story that is often used in talking about, writing about or representing those who have been forced out of their homes and subjugated to various forces and barriers as they trek their way to safety. By doing so, it aims to challenge the universalizing representation of forcibly displaced persons as refugees which creates 'the refugee figure', a figure that has no agency and is identical in his/her experiences to other refugees. Rather, the article aims to counter 'the refugee figure' based upon the premise that each person has his or her singular and unique stories and experiences that cannot be neatly reduced to statistics and numbers. While Abdi's story can be offered as a generic refugee story or even a Somali refugee story, we must not overlook the uniquely contextualized moments that are particular to Abdi and his individual story of struggle, survival and perseverance. To understand these myriad moments that have shaped Abdi's long journey, I rely on the feminist geopolitical critique as a way to unpack the 'unequal and often violent' social relations that operate at both much finer and coarser scales than nation-states (Dowler and Sharp 2001; Hyndman 2004; Massaro and Williams 2013).

To contextualize Abdi's story, the article begins with some background on my encounter with Abdi and his story. I then turn to the theoretical discussion on interconnectedness of place and self. To do so I rely on close reading of Edward Casey's work on *geographical self*. This section attends to the dialectical relations between self and place and the ways by which they mutually shape and are shaped by each other. It then discusses different spatio-temporal vignettes that have shaped Abdi's long path since he left his hometown to his eventual resettlement in Tucson. These vignettes help us better understand how Abdi has related to these different places and how he has negotiated his sense of belonging in various places that he lived since leaving Somalia. I then offer concluding thought on matters of self and place through Abdi's story.

Research Background

In my political geography class, I dedicate a section to forced mobility, displacement and bordering practices that demarcate those who are included and excluded in various socially constructed and politically implicated groups. The class discussions focus on different ways individuals construct, negotiate, challenge and reshape these various walls and bordering practices. After the introductory lecture on that particular section, one of my students asked if he could share his story of leaving his home country and growing up in a refugee camp. The student was Abdi, a soft-spoken young man in a 6-foot frame. He spoke impeccable English and wrote in beautiful cursive – skills, he later told me, he learned in a refugee camp. Abdi was a diligent and thoughtful student who routinely participated in class discussions but other than that I had no knowledge of his background nor was I prepared for this deeply moving and powerful talk. For his talk, Abdi was not given any direction or questions. In spite of our relative positionalities as teacher-student, in that moment and in that space, Abdi commanded the room as he told his story in his own terms. No one but him could impart the deep emotion and affective power of the details of his story. I could teach my class with numbers, infographics, case studies and scholarly references about forced mobility and displacement. But I could not have and still cannot relay the profoundly lived and viscerally experienced moments of Abdi's life to teach students why people are forced to move.

Abdi shared that when he witnessed a carnage on his village, he was about 6 years old. The violence ultimately drove him and his family away from Somalia, his homeland. They left Migwa, a small village in southeastern Somalia and travelled more than 200 miles on foot to reach Kenya. During this treacherous and brutal trip, Abdi watched many people die. Out of initial over 200 who left Migwa with them only about 70 people made it to Kenya. He recalls eventually arriving in Dadaab and by being registered by the UNHCR. Dadaab would be Abdi's home for the next 13 years: "[It is] where I spent half of my life and I grew up and it is where I became a man" (Abdi 2016).

Abdi's story inspired me to start a project on documenting oral histories of people who were forcibly moved from their home countries and are rebuilding their lives in Tucson, Arizona. The original project aimed to counter the growing intolerance and suspicion of refugees both in local and national discourses, specifically in response the Arizona governor's call to halt refugee resettlement in the state at the time. This project has brought the human to the otherwise desensitized, essentializing and all too reductive discourses about individuals who left their homes and homelands because of various circumstances beyond their control. I have since interviewed over 50 individuals who have welcomed me to their homes, offered their food and shared their intimate stories of struggle and survival. Their stories collectively counter the 'danger of single story' of refugees.

When I started my oral history project, Abdi took part and provided a detailed account of his life. In order to disrupt the interviewer-interviewee structure, the interviews followed a semi-structured format to allow him (and other project participants) share as much or a little as he wished. In addition to the semi-structured and recorded formal interviews, Abdi shared pieces of his story in informal settings after which I made extensive notes. Abdi believes that by sharing his story, he can help people better understand why people are forced to flee their homes and homelands. In Adichie's words, he wants to reclaim his nkali or power to shape his story. Abdi's recorded interview is now publicly available. In his words and in his voice, Abdi defines his own story. Ultimately, by sharing his story, he hopes that "people can see, may be tomorrow people will say, it wasn't actually bad to have refugees in the society" (Abdi 2016). In this paper, I do not wish to tell simply retell Abdi's story, but rather to unpack our understanding and assumptions of place and self through Abdi's story.

Theoretical Considerations

Although Abdi left Somalia as a young child and has since never returned, a part of his identity has been intricately tied to this place and has followed him all his life. Yet, he spent most of his life in a refugee camp- a place where he was a perpetual foreigner. And now he is in Tucson where he feels simultaneously belonging and excluded. But what is a place and how do we understand our relations to different places? What does it mean to be displaced? And how do we understand one's sudden and violent rupture from a place? And what if one's sense of place was marred with violence and abuse? Where is home for Abdi anyway?

The connection between a person and a place can manifest on any geographical scale. In understanding people who are forcibly displaced, nation-states are the primary scale of how we conceptualize and regulate human displacement (Hyndman 2000). To belong to a nation-state is to be legible and to be afforded the rights and privileges that come with the legibility. To be outside of this political matrix is to be illegible, stateless or otherwise to exist in a liminal and politically fraught state (Haddad 2008). Jennifer Hyndman refers to this state of exclusion as 'visceral human geography of dislocation' (2000, xv). *Dis*location or *dis*placement is predicated upon the assumption that one is removed from one's rightful location or place – the place to which one feels belongs and for which one has an effective connection.

Geographers have attempted to understand the connection between place and one's identity beyond their attachment to nation-states (Casey 2001; Dempsey 2018, 2020; Massey 1994; Nelson and Hiemstra 2008; Staeheli 2003). Various scholars, especially in humanistic tradition, have regarded places as indispensable to geographical actors (e.g., Tuan 1977; Relph 1976; Sack 1997). "Recognition of place as foundational of the human, and as the medium through which everyday geographic actors negotiate reality, are core themes of humanistic geography" (Davidson 2008, 162). This approach has been critiqued for its tendency to essentialize place and for its lack of consideration of various social and power relations that are inherent in one's experience with places (Rose 1993).

For others place is a messy and slippery concept. For instance, Staeheli (2003) argues that place has not been adequately conceptualized despite its importance and relevance to geographic inquiries. According to her, place is shaped by its relationality to things around and to people that inhabit it. Place is experienced, lived, embodied, and socially mediated. It is continuously negotiated by different actors who perceive, claim, share and use place, and who co-exist or conflict with one another. More importantly, as Staeheli suggests, place has political potential. Place can be mobilized for political purposes and can be both a subject and a tool of political struggles.

Feminist scholars, in particular, have insisted on paying attention to broader social relations and power geometry in studies of place (e.g., Massey 1994; Rose 1993). In understanding how people relate to places they inhabit, we must thus consider an individual's spatio-temporal positionality (recognizing that it can shift over time and space) and relative access to power. As Massey suggests, some inhabit places; some move to and from places and some are imprisoned in them; and these experiences are often racialized and gendered. And places are not static, according to Massey. They can be conceptualized by social relations which are themselves ever-evolving processes: 'what gives a place its specificity is … that it is constructed out of a particular constellation of social relations, meeting and weaving together at a particular locus' (Massey 1994, 154).

In understanding Abdi's journey from Migwa to Tucson, Massey's invitation to see places as the constellations of social relations is helpful. They help understand various local and global forces that operate to serve some while oppressing others. But we must be also careful of using the God's-eye view of trans-local social networks in understanding "the everyday, lived and felt geographies of less omniscient subjects" (Davidson 2008, 165). Zooming out (as in Massey's satellite image peering down the earth) to understand the complex social networks, we might risk of overlooking individuals' sensory, kinaesthetic and affective connections to places they inhabit (Myadar and Davidson 2020).

I thus turn to Casey (2001), who proposes to consider *place* as dialectical to *self* and each is essential to the being of the other. Human subject is oriented and situated in place and he calls this human subject a 'geographical self'. For Casey, the dialectical relation between place and self is thoroughly enmeshed and intimate (2001, 407). He argues *'there is no place without self and no self without place'* (2001, 684). It is a type of mutual engagement and embeddedness marked by persistent qualities of the other. Place and self are tied together what Casey calls *habitus*. 'Human beings act on the basis of habitus, and action is something that is both lived … and intentional' (2001, 687). This relationship, according to Casey, is "not just one of reciprocal influence … but also, more radically, of constitutive coingredience" (2001, 406).

Even transient places, as Casey suggests, can have lasting impacts on the self. Casey (2001, 414) writes:

> Places come into us lastingly; once having been in a particular place for any considerable time- or even briefly, if our experience there has been intense- we are forever marked by that place, which lingers in us indefinitely and in a thousand ways, many too attenuated to specify.

Building upon the existing scholarship on the immanence of place to self, the article contributes to the less-understood aspect of the connection between self and place – the rupture of self from a place. If place and self are so deeply and thoroughly enmeshed, how do we understand the violent rupture of self from a place? What does it mean to be marked by those places that come to us lastingly, if one's experience with the place was violent and fraught?

On Being from Somalia

Abdi's displacement from Somalia a country of his birth was sudden and violent. This vignette situates Abdi's story within a broader geopolitical context and various threads that have helped to weave the story of contemporary Somalia.

'I am originally from Somalia', is how Abdi often introduces himself. Although he fled Somalia when he was only 6 years old, his identity has been tied to Somalia as he has navigated various bureaucratic and administrative grids and hurdles throughout his life. Somalia gave a context to both his displacement and resettlement.

Located along the coast of east Africa, Somalia has been plagued by violence and instability since the country descended into a civil war in the early nineties. Often referred to as the case of a 'failed state', Somalia accompanies assumptions related to anarchism, pirates and terrorists in political and popular imaginary. '[B]ecoming another Somalia is the fate to be avoided by every African state' (Luling 1997, 287). Reinforcing this popular imaginary, the US has imposed a travel ban on Somalia despite the fact that to date no American life has been lost on US soil because of a terrorist attack committed by citizens of Somalia.

To understand the state of contemporary Somalia, we must reckon with various geopolitical forces that have played some role in fashioning the political, social and cultural geographies of the country, many of which have been external to Somalia. During the colonial era, as colonial powers shifted between Britain, Italy, France and Ethiopia, the fates of those who inhabited the territory were shaped by a mix of colonial political violence, scientific racism and imperial hegemony (Besteman 1996; Lewis 1994; Luling 1997).

Despite the country gaining independence in 1960, post-colonial Somalia continued to be subjected to various external forces. Because of the country's strategic location and natural harbours, Somalia was considered a significant geopolitical interest to both the Soviet and US governments with each party providing military aid and weapons at different points in history (Brind 1983; Mohamed 2009). In 1969, the president of Somalia, Abdirashid Ali Shermarke, was assassinated by one of his bodyguards, leaving a sudden power vacuum. Shermarke's top army officer, General Mohammed Siad Barre, subsequently clenched power in a bloodless coup d'état who would go on to rule the country for the next two decades (Menkhaus 2014).

During his long reign, Barre attempted to eliminate tensions among clan-based groups, officially banning various symbolic and material expressions of clannism in 1971 (Lewis 1994). But the Barre regime faced increasing resistance from armed clan groups in the 1980s and his rule would end in 1991 by the very forces he had hoped to eliminate. The country immediately descended into a state of violent chaos and carnage.

The proliferation of weapons in Somalia supplied by the Soviet and US governments would make the fate of post-Cold War Somalia especially precarious. With different-armed groups fighting for the control of the country, violence became widespread. The Somali economy collapsed, and the years of conflict destroyed the country's crops. Thousands of Somalis lost their lives and thousands of others fled the country. Catastrophic famine haunted those who remained as vividly described in Jane Perlez's (1992) award winning report on the crisis. During the famine, children were the most vulnerable and thousands lost their lives during these years.

In the god's eye view, these large-scale geopolitical, power and social relations certainly played an important role in shaping not only Somalia's fate but Abdi's fate as an individual. But these scales cannot adequately capture the intimate details that are specific to Abdi's story. Abdi was a young child during this time and witnessed gruesome violence firsthand. The vivid details of his memory of the violence and lasting abject pain he has since experienced since cannot be captured by the god's eye view.

To borrow from Casey, Somalia, as a place comes to Abdi everlastingly, even though his rupture from Somalia was sudden and violent. To Abdi, rather than the broader geopolitical conditions, it was that particular tragic day was the reason why he and his remaining family had to leave Somalia. As he spent the next 14 years in refugee camps (13 years in Dadaab and 1 year in Kakuma refugee camps) in neighbouring Kenya, Abdi's prospect of returning to Migwa once he called home became more distant; as would his memories of the place he left as a young boy outside that particular day that etched into his memory so vividly. Because of this memory, Abdi said: "If there was peace in Somalia, I don't think I can go back to Somalia: To me my mother being shot in an execution style still lingers in my head."

On Being the Other

I was being targeted being a minority. I was always looked down as a slave. They called me worst possible names imaginable (Abdi 2016).

Somalia was that particular place that cradled Abdi upon birth. Yet, it was a place where he never fully belonged and from which he was violently driven away. What does it mean to be marked as different and to be treated as inferior in a place that is permanently attached to one's identity?

While different historical moments contributed to the process of making Abdi (and millions of others) a refugee, presenting Somalia as a singular entity ontologically and epistemologically obscures the complexities and contradictions within it. The Somali social landscape is as rich and complex as its history and various people who have called it home.

During his interviews, Abdi often referred to his struggle as a refugee in the context of 'his people's struggle'. The people, to whom Abdi refers as 'my people', are communities of peoples that are part of the Somalian nation but are marginalized due to their particular positionality as the Other (Besteman 1996), produced and perpetuated by historically contextualized and socially sanctioned perception of differences between Abdi and 'his people' and the rest of Somalian ethos.

Much attention has been devoted to the clan-based tensions as the root cause of Somalia's contemporary political conditions (Lewis 1998; Luling 1997; 2006; Hesse 2010). Focusing on the clan-based nature of contemporary Somalian conflict perpetuates the idea that Somalia otherwise is a fairly homogenous society, 'free from the ethnic divisions that plague nearly all the others with a single culture, language and religion' (Luling 1997, 287). According to Lewis (2004), the differences that define the Somali rival groups are thus 'invisible', unlike the ethnically, culturally, linguistically or religiously rooted 'visible differences' that are common elsewhere.

While understanding Somalian social tapestry through a clan-based lens is not inherently wrong, focusing solely on the clan system would fail to appreciate the geographies of violence and discrimination experienced by those who are outside the domains of clan-based tensions in Somalia.

Abdi refers to himself as a Somali *Jareer*. Somali *Jareer* (alternatively known as Bantu1993 or Gosha)[2] are the descendants of many ethnic groups who were brought to the area of today's Somalia in the 19th century as slaves within the broader East African slave trade industry. Literally meaning hard-hair (as opposed to *Jilaac* or soft hair), the Jareer community embodies the lived experience of discrimination and systemic oppression. Jareer thus is a politically inscribed and socially constructed identity ascribed to a disparate group of people whose ancestors hailed from various African communities but are united in their shared experience of historical subjugation and ongoing mistreatment and marginalization. Despite the fact that Abdi and his people considered themselves full citizens of the Somali society with common language, religion and cultural background, they were considered as distinct and inferior to others in Somalia. Pointing to his hair, Abdi said, 'you see my hair is kinky and my skin is dark. That is why they didn't like us' (Abdi 2018).

Anthropologist Catherine Besteman (1991) provides important context to the formation of Jareer social identity in Somalia. As she argues, fugitive and freed slaves began to settle in the uninhabited territories along the Jubba River Valley establishing their villages over time. Separate villages reflected different tribal and ancestral backgrounds, many of which continued their distinct languages and cultural practices, using Swahili as a lingua franca (Besteman 1991, 108). Over time these villagers began to build closer ties to the Somali clans than the communities of their ancestors in East and Central Africa, adopting Somali language, religion and cultural practices as a way of life (Besteman 1991, 1996; Menkhaus 2014). But the historic mistreatment of the slaves would continue despite the fact the slavery ended and freed slaves would be incorporated within the broader Somali social geography.

The race-based discrimination of Jareer communities would become institutionalized during the colonial era, making Jareer communities a distinct group of an inferior race compared to other Somalis. Colonial authorities designated the area the Jareer communities inhabited as Goshaland, a separate political and administrative unit detached from the rest of Somalia. The people of the Goshaland were singled out in conscription to forced labour campaigns during the fascist rule of Italy (Besteman 1991). By the time Somalia gained independence in 1960, this racial structure that had been slowly superimposing on the Somali nation was firmly cemented. In spite of the relative peace the country experienced following its independence, social marginalization of the

Jareer community persisted. The banality of the violence of marginalization and discrimination against the Jareer communities would erupt into spectacular violence during the civil war. Little Abdi, his family and his community would experience this violence first hand, perpetrated by the people who shared the same Somali citizenship.

While millions of Somalis experienced the wraths of the civil war and famine indiscriminately, the minority groups faced a far greater risk of violence. Because of historically constructed and socially ingrained animosity towards the Jareer community, various militia groups were united in their disregard and contempt for the lives of people like Abdi. Not only had their bodies been marked as Other and but their lives had been considered as not grievable (Butler 2004). In recalling the carnage that he witnessed in his village, he said that 'his people' could not defend themselves because they were not armed like the militia men. He said the attackers wanted his village's land as it was more fertile than theirs[3] (Abdi 2018). The violence is what drove Abdi from his village- the only place he had known until that time. But he had been marked as the Other long before that fateful day.

In sharing his story, Abdi gives a context to the uniquely experienced struggles he and his community endured. This is important to our understanding of place and self. In spite of the immanence of place to self, each geographical actor encounters a place differently and pliantly. Each actor's encounter with a place is thickly layered with experiences unique to them. By allowing us to hear his story, Abdi helps us better understand a subjective and fraught relations we have with places around us.

On Seeking Refuge: refugee Camp and Open Prison

> *From my village to Kenya we walked nearly 30 days. From about 200 people left only about 70 made to the Kenyan border. This was a horrible experience and it was extremely hard. Lots of people died on the way. Some people drank their urine just to survive. But we made it. When we came to the Kenyan border we were registered by the UNHCR. We were transported to the refugee camp where I lived half of my life. It is called Dadaab refugee camp, that is where I grew up and that is where I became a man* (Abdi 2016).

Abdi spent 13 years in Dadaab refugee camp in Kenya before moving to Kakuma refugee camp 2004. Dadaab is the largest refugee camp in the world, hosting about 235,269 people as of January 2018 (UNHCR 2018). How do we understand Abdi's relations with this place to which he arrived to escape violence but in which his life continued to be at a peril?

Place, as Casey suggests, carries 'the immediate ambience of [one's] lived body' (2001, 404). The ambience is the sedimented history that composes one's life story (2001, 404). Abdi is now in his late 30s; he spent half of it in a refugee camp. His life story at the camp provides a nuanced context to the broader understanding of Dadaab beyond a physical site and material location or even its intended meaning. 'It was like an open prison because you can move freely but there was nowhere you can escape to' Abdi said of Dadaab (Abdi 2018). To understand the sedimented history that composed Abdi's encounter with a refugee camp, Abdi's referring to it as an open prison moves it from its reified place to a subjectively experienced and individually situated site.

Abdi's comment regarding the refugee camp challenges various spatio-temporal assumptions related to refugee camps. A refugee camp is defined as 'a temporary space in which refugees may receive humanitarian relief and protection until a durable solution can be found to their situation' (Ramadan 2013, 65). Yet to Abdi, it was an open prison where he was both free and chained.

First, Abdi's likening of refugee camps to prisons suggests that a refugee camp is a place of human detention rather than a place of freedom. Refugees are chained by their status as refugees and cannot leave the camps freely or integrate into the local community because of their lack of legal recognition in the host countries. Giorgio Agamben (1998) regards this *a state of exception* where refugees, as biopolitical subjects, are reduced to bare life. While Agamben is right about the violent nature of the camp infrastructure where the bodies of forcibly displaced people are regulated and disciplined, as scholars note, he does not attend to the agency of the people who challenge, subvert and otherwise resist the rigid confines of the camp symbolically and physically (e.g., Bargu 2017; Mountz 2011).

Abdi's insight also sheds light on the temporality of refugee camps. Abdi's experience defies the assumption that refugee camps are transitional both in the spatial and temporal senses. While it is easy to conceive of refugee camps as temporary space, for most refugees it is a space of constant uncertainty with no immediate prospect of going back or going forward. For many refugees, especially young generations, the camps are their homes, the only place they have ever known.[4]

Abdi's story sheds important light on how place is experienced singularly and uniquely, defined by complex social landscapes within the place. Perhaps more importantly, Abdi's reference to the refugee camp illuminates its ontological ambiguity. It is easy to assume that the camps are places of refuge for people who have fled life-threatening situations in their places of origin. But as Abdi's story reveals, for Abdi and other socially vulnerable individuals, the precariousness of life defined their very existence. During our interview, Abdi talked about how as a minority, he and his family were subjects of routine violence. When Abdi and his family fled Somalia from the violence perpetuated by other Somalis, discrimination and marginalization followed them to Dadaab. "Being a minority, I was always being targeted" Abdi recalled. While those connected with powerful clans or political elites in Somalia fare comparatively well, anyone with minimum social capital, such as minority groups, women, children, the disabled and newcomers are subjected to widespread and persistent violence.

Abdi, for instance, recalled his daily challenges in going to school. 'Being a minority was always a problem ... as a minority they didn't want us to get a better education ... and they called me worst names possible they can think of and I was always being looked as a slave' (Abdi 2016). He endured physical and emotional threats because he was determined that education was the only way out of the grinding and perilous life in the refugee camp. And persist he did. He pushed against the systematic violence and discrimination that he faced. It was a type of agency and resilience that have been noted by various scholars who argue that refugees and displaced persons routinely engage in counter-hegemonic protests (e.g., Mountz 2011; Ramadan 2013; Caraus 2018). And it was his perseverance that helped him and his family eventually leave the camp and rebuild his life in the United States.

As Minca (2015) suggests, the camp constitutes a space 'where the threshold between life and death, and the qualification of a life-worth-living is constantly negotiated'. By listening to stories like Abdi, we can understand and appreciate the nuanced, layered, lived and experienced meanings of places such as a refugee camp. Abdi's story helps untangle fraught relations between self and place. No matter how much one spends in a place, if that place is a source of tension and violence rather than solace and safety, the habitudinal bond between self and place would necessarily be complex. Despite the fact, Dadaab is where Abdi spent most of his life, it never felt home as he never felt rooted in or effectively bonded with it.

Conclusion: on Being at Home

Tucson is home for me, I feel like I belong here now (Abdi 2016)

An individual's very being is routinely tied in the traditional geopolitical discourses and assumptions predicated upon the sanctity of the nation-states. As millions of people are forcibly displaced, they traverse the rigid political boundaries that come with the assumption. Feminist geopolitics offer us a way to see beyond the rigid boundaries of nation-states in order to attend to the embodied, lived, intimate and everyday experiences of people and their situated realities in any given time/space intersection. It also allows us to see the changing, hybrid and intersectional places as we negotiate our place in the world.

Through Abdi's story, this article has sought to contribute to geographic understanding of the immanence of place to self as it relates to displacement and forced mobility. By doing so, it has aimed to challenge the assumption of the dialectical nature of place and self that is so thoroughly enmeshed and intimate as Casey suggests. Rather, the article has sought to push geographic understanding of rupture, especially one that is violent, of self from a place. Abdi's story provides more nuanced context to our relations with places which we inhabit and how these relations are much more fluid and porous than the assumption of 'geographical self'- self that is deeply rooted in and defined by places. This approach reclaims human agency in the dyadic connection between place and self and centres individual experience in geographic study of forced mobility and displacement. No person's experience is the same as the experience of another. Only by hearing individual stories, can we collectively push against generalizing, simplifying or homogenizing disparate experiences of people who have been forced to move because of reasons beyond their control.

Abdi's story has helped me to be attentive to the single and unique struggles of individuals who have been forcibly displaced and are seeking to build their homes wherever they might be. Through Abdi's story, the article has aimed to decentre the totalizing discourse about displaced peoples across the world today and move away from the 'danger of single story' of refugees to return to Adichie. It moves from the 'refugee figure' who is seen as a problem to be solved within the nation-state-based global refugee regime to understanding each individual's story of fighting for the fundamental human right for safety and peace. The article weaved together situated experiences of Abdi, not as a representative of *a refugee figure*, rather as a way to demonstrate the embodied, singular and lived story of one man who has negotiated these various scales as he trekked a long way from one spatial/temporal point to the next.

To return to the discussion on the intersection of place and self, we must consider its 'highly-contested and open-ended' nature of one's habitudinal bond with any place. The bond is shaped not only by complex power dynamics and broader social relations but also individuals' particular positionalities within these dynamics. But more importantly, it is the individual's affective connection, intimate relations and viscerally experienced moments that shape and define this bond.

Abdi's story and his journey from Migwa to Tucson illustrate the nomad potential of his connection and disconnection to various places he has inhabited. He is not moored to a place but he lives in one place without closing the potential for another. Casey (2000, 186) suggests 'the place is there to be re-entered by the memory if not by bodily movement.' Somalia is attached to Abdi's identity, yet it is a distant place both spatially and symbolically. Somalia 're-enters' Abdi through the vivid images that pushed him away rather than draw him towards it. He has also fraught connections to Kenya where he spent most of his life. And he is still negotiating his sense of belonging and connection to Tucson where he has built his home since he arrived in 2005. After graduating from the university, the first in his family to graduate from college, he began running an African store with his extended family members. He is now married and a father of seven children.

Tucson feels like home to Abdi – more than any other places he has ever lived. He is grateful that when he wakes up in the morning he knows that his family is safe. But he is also aware of the continued challenges faced by him and his family. During one of my recent interviews, he expressed his uneasiness with the rising anti-Muslim and anti-immigrant sentiment that was echoed in Trump's executive orders and the travel ban on his country of birth (Abdi 2018). As Mountz and Hiemstra suggest (2014), this speaks to the sovereign power of marking certain bodies as security threats to be criminalized, securitized and excluded. 'I know evil people out there. But not everybody is bad. You cannot punish whole community for one bad apple, and for one person … It is not fair' (Abdi 2016). By telling his story, Abdi pushes against this sovereign power and reclaims his *nkali* to shape his own story.

Notes

1. When Abdi introduced himself for the first time, he told me I could call him Abdi. He did not ask to be anonymous or to alter his name in this publication.
2. Besteman (1991) argues that *Jareer* is a derogatory term and prefers Gosha instead. In my interviews, however, Abdi referred himself as *Jareer* and out of respect to his self-identity I will use the term *Jareer* in this paper.
3. To put Abdi's comment in context, the *Jareer* communities live along in the inter-riverine area of southern Somalia along two rivers, Shabelle and Juba. Compared to other areas in Somalia, this region is more arable owing to its temperate climate and higher precipitation.
4. In Dadaab 1000 babies are were born at the camp every month (Rawlence 2016).

Acknowledgments

I wish to thank Editor Nancy Hiemstra and anonymous reviewers for their constructive comments and feedback. My deepest thanks goes to Abdi for sharing his life story with me and allowing me to share it with others.

Funding

The research for this article was generously funded by the Confluencenter for Creative Inquiry, Tucson, Arizona.

ORCID

Orhon Myadar http://orcid.org/0000-0002-0372-2960

References

Abdi. 2016. *Personal interview. Recorded on May 05, 2016*. University of Arizona, Tucson, Arizona.
Abdi. 2018. *Personal interview. Recorded on September 08, 2018*. University of Arizona, Tucson, Arizona.
Adichie, C. N., 2009. The danger of a single story. Accessed September 13, 2019. https://www.ted.com/talks/chimamanda_ngozi_adichie_the_danger_of_a_single_story.
Agamben, G. 1998. *Homo sacer: Sovereign power and bare life*. Stanford: Stanford University Press.
Bargu, B. 2017. The silent exception: Hunger striking and lip-sewing. *Law, Culture and the Humanities* 1743872117709684.
Besteman, C. 1996. Representing violence and 'othering' Somalia. *Cultural Anthropology* 11 (1):120–33. doi:10.1525/can.1996.11.1.02a00060.
Besteman, C. L., 1991. Land tenure, social power, and the legacy of slavery in southern Somalia. Doctoral Dissertation. University of Arizona.
Brind, H. 1983. Soviet policy in the Horn of Africa. *International Affairs (Royal Institute of International Affairs 1944-)* 60 (1):75–95.
Butler, J. 2004. *Precarious life: The powers of mourning and violence*. New York: Verso Books.
Caraus, T. 2018. Migrant protests as acts of cosmopolitan citizenship. *Citizenship Studies* 22 (8):791–809.
Casey, E. S. 2001. Between geography and philosophy: What does it mean to be in the place-world ?. Annals of the Association of American Geographers, 91(4) 683–93.
Casey, E.S., 2000. Remembering: A phenomenological study. Indiana University Press, Bloomington, IN
Davidson, R. A. 2008. Recalcitrant space: Modeling variation in humanistic geography. *Journal of Cultural Geography* 25 (2):161–80.
Dempsey, K. E. 2018. Negotiated positionalities and ethical considerations of fieldwork on migration: Interviewing the interviewer. *ACME: An International Journal for Critical Geographies* 17 (1):88–108.
Dempsey, K. E. 2020. Spaces of violence: A typology of the political geography of violence against migrants seeking asylum in the EU. *Political Geography*. 72:102–57.
Dowler, L., and J. Sharp. 2001. A feminist geopolitics? *Space and Polity* 5 (3):165–76.
Haddad, E. 2008. *The refugee in international society: Between sovereigns*, Vol. 106. Cambridge, UK: Cambridge University Press.
Hesse, B. J. 2010. Introduction: The myth of Somalia. *Journal of Contemporary African Studies* 28 (3):247–59. doi:10.1080/02589001.2010.499232.
Hyndman, J. 2000. *Managing displacement: Refugees and the politics of humanitarianism*. University of Minnesota Press, Minneapolis, Minnesota.

Hyndman, J. 2004. Mind the gap: Bridging feminist and political geography through geopolitics. *Political Geography* 23 (3):307–22. doi:10.1016/j.polgeo.2003.12.014.

Jones, R. 2016. *Violent borders: Refugees and the right to move*. Brooklyn, NY: Verso Books.

Lewis, I. M. 1994. *Blood and bone: The call of kinship in Somali society*. Lawrenceville, NJ: The Red Sea Press.

Lewis, I. M. 1998. Doing violence to ethnography: A response to Catherine Besteman's 'Representing violence and 'othering' Somalia'. *Cultural Anthropology* 13:1008.

Lewis, I. M. 2004. Visible and invisible differences: The Somali paradox. *Africa* 74 (4):489514. doi:10.3366/afr.2004.74.4.489.

Luling, V. 1997. Come back Somalia? Questioning a collapsed state. *Third World Quarterly* 18 (2):287–302. doi:10.1080/01436599714957.

Luling, V., 2006. Genealogy as Theory, Genealogy as Tool: Aspects of Somali 'Clanship'. Social Identities, 12(4), pp.471–485 doi:10.1080/13504630600823692

Massaro, V. A., and J. Williams. 2013. Feminist geopolitics. *Geography Compass* 7 (8):567–77. doi:10.1111/gec3.12054.

Massey, D. 1994. *Space, place and gender*. Minneapolis: University of Minnesota Press.

Menkhaus, K. 2014. Calm between the storms? Patterns of political violence in Somalia, 1950–1980. *Journal of Eastern African Studies* 8 (no. 4):558–72.

Minca, C. 2015. Geographies of the camp. *Political Geography* 49:74–83. doi:10.1016/j.polgeo.2014.12.005.

Mohamed, M. A. 2009. *US strategic interest in Somalia: From Cold War era to war on terror*. Buffalo: State University of New York.

Mountz, A. 2011. Where asylum-seekers wait: Feminist counter-topographies of sites between states. *Gender, Place & Culture* 18 (3):381–99. doi:10.1080/0966369X.2011.566370.

Mountz, A., and N. Hiemstra. 2014. Chaos and crisis: Dissecting the spatiotemporal logics of contemporary migrations and state practices. *Annals of the Association of American Geographers* 104 (2):382–90. doi:10.1080/00045608.2013.857547.

Myadar, O., and R. A. Davidson. 2020. "Mom, I want to come home": Geographies of compound displacement, violence and longing. *Geoforum* 109:78–85.

Nelson, L., and N. Hiemstra. 2008. Latino immigrants and the renegotiation of place and belonging in small town America. *Social & Cultural Geography* 9 (3):319–42. doi:10.1080/14649360801990538.

Perlez, J. December 07, 1992. Deaths in Somalia outpace delivery of food. NewYork: *New York Times*.

Ramadan, A. 2013. Spatialising the refugee camp. *Transactions of the Institute of British Geographers* 38 (1):65–77. doi:10.1111/j.1475-5661.2012.00509.x.

Rawlence, B. 2016. *City of thorns: Nine lives in the world's largest refugee camp*. NewYork: Picador.

Relph, E., 1976. Place and placelessness (Vol. 67). London: Pion

Rose, G. 1993. *Feminism & geography: The limits of geographical knowledge*. University of Minnesota Press, Minneapolis, Minnesota.

Sack, R.D., 1997. Homo geographicus: A framework for action, awareness, and moral concern. Baltimore: Johns Hopkins University Press

Staeheli, L. 2003. Place. In *A companion to political geography*, ed. J. Agnew, K. Mitchell, and G. Toal, 158–70. Oxford: Blackwell.

Tuan, Y. 1977. *Space and place: The perspective of experience*. University of Minnesota Press, Minneapolis, Minnesota.

UNHCR. 2018. Accessed February 8 2019. https://www.unhcr.org/.

Index

Page numbers in **bold** refer to tables and those in *italic* refer to figures.

Abdi, the story: on being the other 103–5; refugee camp and open prison 105–7; research background 98–9; from Somalia 101–3; theoretical 99–101
Adichie, Chimamanda Ngozi 97
advocacy networks 39
Agamben, Giorgio 106
'age of terrorism' 15
Alien Police (AVIM) 42
Allen, W. 13, 15
Amarasingam, A. 64
Amnesty International 51
Anderson, B. 13, 15
Andersson, R. 83
anti-essentialism 62
antifoundationalism 62
anti-government backlash and 2015/2016 28–9
antirepresentation 62
'anxious politics' 90
The Aquarius case 85
Arab Spring 17
Arendt, Hannah 3
Ashutosh, I. 23, 26
asylum applications, Netherlands (2013–2015) *38*
asylum camps 40–1
asylum seekers 24, 37–8, 42–7, 83
Asylum Seekers Alliance of Keipelgevangenis Camp (2016) 36

Bauder, H. 16
Berns-McGown, R. 62, 65
Besteman, Catherine 104
Bleiker, R. 80
Blended Sponsorship Refugee (BSR) program 22
Boundaries and Territories and Postmodernity 1
Bradley, M. 12
Braghiroli, S. 16
Bretherton, L. 85
Brigden, N. 79, 82
Brun, C. 47
bureaucratic processes 37

'the cage' 64
camp ambassadors 41
Campbell, D. 80
Canadian and US resettlement systems 22
Canadian general election (2015) 11
The Canadian model 21
Canadian nationalists 23
care: legislative frameworks 83–5; and migration 81–3
Carter, S. 62
Carvalho, A. 80
Casey, E. S. 97, 101, 105, 108
Castañeda, H. 16
Chavez, L. 15
Chimamanda Ngozi Adichie's concept 6
civil wars 11–12, **18**
the Cold War 13
collective agency 49
colonial authorities 104
community members 10
comprehensive security checks 65
Corcoran, Ann 28
Corriere della Sera newspaper 89
counter-hegemonic efforts 47–8
Cresswell, T. 62
Cuttitta, P. 86

"danger of a single story" (2009) 97
Davidson, J. 81
decolonization 13
Dench, Janet 66
Departure International Service (DT&V) 43
diaspora geopolitics: defined 58; minority ethnonational groups 60; mobility and 62–4; personal and geopolitical processes 59; Tamil nationalism 60; transnational politics 58
'dislocated temporality' 39
diverse insurgencies 13
domestic immigration debates 10
'dublined' individuals 84
Dublin III Regulation 2013 42
Dublin system 84, 90
Dutch asylum camps 5, 37

Dutch Border Police 42
Dutch Central Agency 43
Dutch Immigration and Naturalisation Service (IND) 43
Dutch immigration laws 45–6, 48
Dutch Koepelgevangenis asylum camp 48
Dutch Repatriation 43
Düvell, F. 13, 15

economic and environmental shocks 17
'economic migrant' 3
Edict of Nantes (1685) 2
ethnic communities 17
ethnic conflicts 11–12
European States, role of 88–90

Fabos, C. 47
family reunification 24
feminist geographers 47
feminist geopolitics 39, 41
Fischer-Lescano, A. 83, 89
Fisher, B. 79
foreign policy goals 10
'Fortress Europe' policies 22

Gardiner Expressway 64–5
Geneva Convention (1951) 52
geographers 81, 100
Gilbert, G. 15
The Global Forced Migration Crisis 11–17
globally-displaced populations 3
governmental officials 23–4
Government-Assisted Refugees (GAR) 22
Government of Sri Lanka (GoSL) 59, 61
grassroots non-violent securities 39
Greater Toronto Area (GTA) 62, 64, 66
The *Guardian* (2010) 65
Gulf countries 17
Gupte, J. 2

Harper, Stephen 61
health outreach listservs 66
Held, V. 81
Hero's Day (*Maveerar Naal*) 69
Hiemstra, N. 109
Holmes, S. 16
Hough, J. 13, 15
humanitarian in Mediterranean 85–8
Human Subjects Protocol 41–2
Humphris, R. 13, 15
Hutchison, E. 80
Hyndman, J. 13, 15, 41, 79, 100

'illegal migrant' 3
Immigration and Refugee Board 59
'immigration control' 23

'immigration policy' 23
The Independent newspaper 90
'internally displaced persons' 13
The International Crisis Group (2020) 59
interview guides 66–7
intrastate geopolitics 43
'involuntary immobility' 63
Islamic State group 17
Islamist forces 17

Jareer communities 105
Jeyeraj, D. B. S. 70
Joppke, C. 14

Keipelgevangenis Camp 44
Kennedy, D. 88

labels, policy-making process 3
'Latino threat narrative' 15
Lawson, V. 81, 82
Lewis, I. M. 103
Liberation Tigers of Tamil Eelam (LTTE) 58–61, 67–9
local social workers 41
Löhr, T. 83, 89
Lough, S. 59

Macron, Emanuel 89
Mainwaring, C. 79, 82
Makarychev, A. 16
"making and unmaking refugees" 2
Malkki, L. 62
Massey, D. 63, 100
McNeely, A. 59
McNevin, A. 50
media reports 37
Medicine Sans Borders (MSF) 86
Mehta, L. 2
migrants' mobility technique 44
Milligan, C. 81
Minca, C. 107
Ministry of Security and Justice (2016) 45–6
Monahan, J. 62, 65
Morden, M. 62, 65
Mountz, A. 23, 26, 79, 82, 83, 84, 109
'Muslim threat narrative' 15

National Support for the Undocumented (LOS) 52
national telephone survey 65
Newman, David 1
new social movements 13
Nicholson, X. 80
nkali principle 97
non-governmental officials 23–4
non-refoulement principle 83
N-VIVO software 66

INDEX

Obama Administration 19, 20, 21, 28
Office of Refugee Resettlement 26–7
Open Door (Wereldhuis) 52
oppression of groups 11–12
'Otherness' migrants 46

Perlez, Jane 102
Petyrna, A. 88
'policy gap' 14
Politics of Refugee Resettlement 11–17
Popke, J. 79
Privately Sponsored Refugees (PSR) 22
Proactiva Open Arms, Spanish NGO vessel 87
Public Safety Canada 61
Pugh, M. 79, 88

reception and placement (R&P) consultations 28
Red Cross employees 41
Refugee Convention (1951) 2
Refugee Resettlement Watch 28
refugees 24; camp 106; definition 2; determination 13; diasporas 63; policies 14; resettlement 20
'Refugees-on-the-Street' 51
Reid-Henry, S. M. 85–8
Republican presidential primaries (2015–2016) 20
Rose, L. 13, 15
Rozakou, K. 85

Safe Third Country Agreement 22
Sajjad, T. 3
Salvini, Matteo 79, 88
sea-borne migrants 90
search and rescue activities (SAR) 6
Sea Watch 89
self-promotion 39
Sheller, M. 62
smugglers 79
social advocacy 49
social media campaigns 39, 49
social service providers 10
Somali *Jareer* 104
Special Immigrant Visa (SIV) program 14
Staeheli, L. 100
Stockemer, D. 16
Sumption, M. 13, 15
Sunni Muslim rebel groups 17
Support Committee for Undocumented Workers (OKIA) 51
Syrian Kurds 18
Syrian refugees 10; crisis 4; desirability of 24–5; and global response 17–19

Tamil Canadians 60; first generation 67; 1.5-generation 67
Tamil community online newspapers 66
Tamil diaspora 67–71
Tamil Displacement 64–6
Tamil National Alliance (TNA) 68
Tamil Student Association (TSA) 66
'Tamil Tigers' *see* Liberation Tigers of Tamil Eelam (LTTE)
Taylor, P. 90
Tazzioli, M. 44, 86
terrorists 46
third countries, Global North 12
Tohidipur, T. 83, 89
Toronto. *see* diaspora geopolitics
Torres, R. 23
traffickers 79
Transnational Government of Tamil Eelam (TGTE) 63
'travel bans' 21
Tronto, J. 79
Trudeau, Justin 11, 22
Turkish Kurds 18

'undeportables' migrants 38, 39, 50–1
UN General Assembly (1967) 2
UN Human Rights Agreement (1948) 12
United Nations Refugee Agency (UNRA) 82
United Nations Refugee Convention (1951) 12, 82
Urry, J. 62
US and Canadian responses 19–22
US–government officials 10
US Refugee Admissions Program (USRAP) 19–20

Van Hear, N. 13, 15, 63
'violent abandonment' 45
visit-related asylum forums 50
Vollmer, B. 16

Waldman, Lorne 65
Walker, S. 13, 15
Wanni region 62
'watch dog agency' 49
Watkins, J. 16
welfare thieves 46
Westphalian categorisations of citizenship 37
Williams, K. 83, 84
World Tamil Movement (WTM) 65

xenophobic rhetorics 25–7

Zetter, R. 82, 83